The ESSENTIALS of

Production & Operations Management

Sai Kolli, Ph.D.
Lecturer
School of Management
University of Texas at Dallas

Research & Education Association
61 Ethel Road West
Piscataway, New Jersey 08854

THE ESSENTIALS®
OF PRODUCTION AND OPERATIONS
MANAGEMENT

Printed in the United States of America

Library of Congress Catalog Card Number 99-75912

International Standard Book Number 0-87891-222-3

WHAT "THE ESSENTIALS" WILL DO FOR YOU

This book is a comprehenensive and concise review of the findings in the field.

It is a handy reference source.

It condenses the vast amount of detail characteristic of the subject matter and summarizes the **essentials** of the field.

It will thus save hours of research and preparation time.

The book provides quick access to the important facts, principles, procedures, and techniques in the field.

Materials needed for this subject can be reviewed in summary form – eliminating the need to read and reread many pages of reference materials. The summaries will even tend to bring detail to mind that had been previously read or noted.

This "ESSENTIALS" book has been prepared by experts in the field, and has been carefully reviewed to assure accuracy and maximum usefulness.

Dr. Max Fogiel
Program Director

CONTENTS

Chapter 6
JUST-IN-TIME PRODUCTION SYSTEM

Chapter 7
CAPACITY PLANNING

Chapter 8
FACILITY LOCATION

Chapter 9
FACILITY LAYOUT

Chapter 10
DESIGN OF WORK SYSTEMS

Chapter 11
PROJECT MANAGEMENT

Chapter 12
AGGREGATE PLANNING

Chapter 13
INVENTORY MANAGEMENT

Chapter 14
MATERIAL REQUIREMENTS PLANNING

CHAPTER 1

Production and Operations Management

Production and operations management is the management of systems or processes that create goods and services. It deals with the design, operation, and improvement of these systems or processes. Operations management is responsible for transforming inputs to an organization into desired outputs. For example, a hospital uses doctors, nurses, medical equipment, and facilities as *inputs*; examination, surgery, medication, and therapy for *transformation*; and produces healthy individuals as the *desired output*.

1.1   Operations Function

Operations management is the most important of the three main functions in any organization: finance, marketing, and operations. Organizations exist to satisfy society's needs for goods and services. The *operations function* is responsible for creating those goods and delivering the services; without operations, there is no reason for the other functions to exist. This core function also controls a major portion of an organization's assets and employs a large number of people in most organizations.

While organizational strategies support the goals and missions of the organization, functional strategies support the organizational strategy. Operations strategy deals with the formulation of policies and plans for effectively using production resources to support the organizational strategy.

For operations to become a positive contributing factor to organizational success, the following steps should be used to link organizational strategy and operations:

1. Analyze the competitive situation (external environment).

2. Appraise the skills and resources of the organization.

3. Formulate the organizational strategy.

4. Determine implications of organizational strategy on operations.

5. Examine the limitations of economics and technology on operations.

6. Design systems for operations.

7. Develop plans for operations.

8. Monitor and control operations.

1.2 Classification of Operations

Operations are classified into manufacturing or service based on the type of output, either goods or services. Manufacturing implies production of tangible output (e.g., automobiles, radios, or golf balls). Service implies delivery of an act (e.g., doctor's exam, lawn care, showing a film, or teaching a course at school). Manufacturing is product-oriented and service is act-oriented.

The primary differences between manufacturing and service operations are shown in the following chart:

2

	Manufacturing	Service
Output	Tangible	Intangible
Customer contact	Low	High
Uniformity of input and output	High	Low
Labor content	Low	High
Measurement of productivity	Easy	Difficult
Inventory	Yes	No

1.3 Productivity

Productivity is used to measure effectiveness of the usage of resources (human, equipment, facilities, etc.) to produce goods and services. It is an index expressed as a ratio of output to input.

$$\text{Productivity} = \frac{\text{Production output}}{\text{Input}}$$

Productivity is also expressed in terms of the production elements: labor, facilities, and raw materials.

$$\text{Labor productivity} = \frac{\text{Production output}}{\text{Labor input}}$$

$$\text{Facility productivity} = \frac{\text{Production output}}{\text{Facility input}}$$

$$\text{Raw material productivity} = \frac{\text{Production output}}{\text{Raw material input}}$$

These measures are called single-factor productivity measures. *Total productivity*, a multi-factor productivity measure, is based on a combination of inputs using a common unit of measurement, such as cost and value.

$$\text{Total productivity} = \frac{\text{Quantity of production at standard price}}{\text{Cost of labor, facilities, and raw materials}}$$

A productivity index is useful for tracking performance over time and helping decide where improvements are needed. Factors that affect productivity include production methods, capital, quality, technology, and management.

1.4 Competitiveness

Competitiveness refers to how effective an organization is in the market compared to other organizations that offer similar goods or services. It is an important factor in determining the success or failure of an organization. Price, quality, time, product differentiation, and flexibility are some of the attributes that are used in designing competitive strategies.

CHAPTER 2

Quality Management/Quality Control

In a broad sense, quality pertains to the ability of a product or service to meet or exceed the expectations of a customer. From a customer's perspective, quality refers to *value*—how well the product serves its intended purpose—and from the producer's perspective, it refers to *conformance to specifications*. Quality does not refer to a single aspect of the product but to several dimensions of the product, such as conformance, reliability, durability, performance, and service after sale.

Organizations that offer products with good quality have increased sales, market share, goodwill, and competitive strength. Poor quality products cause:

1. Damage to the organization's image, reduced market share, etc.

2. Increased liability expenses due to damages or injuries to the customer.

3. Lower productivity due to extra time spent on inspection, repairs, etc.

4. Increased costs for inspection, scrap, rework, warranty, repair, etc.

2.1 Quality Costs

The costs involved in quality management may be classified into four categories:

1. *Internal failure costs* are a result of failures during the production process due to reasons such as defective materials, faulty equipment settings, and incorrect procedures. Included in this category are scrap, rework, repair, inspection costs, and additional labor costs.

2. *External failure costs* are a result of failures after the product is delivered to the customer. These costs include warranty, cost of handling complaints, and returned merchandise.

3. *Appraisal costs* are a result of activities to detect defective products. Included in this category are costs for inspection, testing, laboratories, equipment, and audits.

4. *Prevention costs* are a result of activities to identify the cause of a defect and implement corrective action to prevent defects from occurring. These costs include planning and administrative costs, training personnel, and design improvements.

2.2 Quality Awards/Standards

The Malcolm Baldrige Award, administered by the U.S. National Institute for Standards and Technology, is awarded annually to recognize quality achievements and to stimulate efforts to improve quality. Past recipients include Motorola and Federal Express.

The Deming Prize, a Japanese award, is given annually to recognize successful efforts to institute company-wide quality control principles. Past recipients include Toyota and Florida Power and Light. While the major focus of the Baldrige Award is on overall customer satisfaction, the Deming Prize focuses on statistical quality control.

The ISO 9000 Standard, administered by the International Standardization Organization, is a series of quality standards, numbered from 9000 to 9004, for activities ranging from design and development to procurement, production, installation, and servicing. Companies attempt to receive ISO 9000 certification and registration to establish quality management systems within the company, to enhance their competitive edge, and to deal with the global marketplace.

2.3 Other Quality Topics

1. *Total Quality Management (TQM)* is a philosophy that involves everyone in the organization in a quest for quality, with customer satisfaction as the driving force and the customer as the focal point. The TQM approach involves the following main aspects:

   a. Finding out about the customer's requirements.

   b. Designing a product/service that will meet/exceed the customer's expectations.

   c. Designing a "mistake-proof" process.

   d. Monitoring the process, keeping track of results, and using them to guide improvement, not ceasing the efforts to improve.

   e. Extending these concepts to suppliers and to the distribution function.

2. *Continuous improvement* (also referred to as *Kaizen*) is a philosophy involving "never-ending" efforts to improve the process of converting inputs to outputs.

3. *Pareto analysis* involves classification and ranking of problem areas (defects, complaints, etc.) based on the degree of importance, and then focusing on the most important problem.

4. *Quality circle* refers to a group of employees who meet periodically to discuss methods to improve products and processes.

5. *Brainstorming* is a technique for generating a free flow of ideas from a group of employees on a particular topic, such as identifying problem areas, causes for a defect, and methods to improve a process.

6. *Benchmarking* is used to establish a standard against which performance is judged. This process involves:

   a. Identifying an item or operation that needs improvement.

   b. Identifying an organization or product that is the best.

   c. Studying the best product or operation and establishing a benchmark.

   d. Improving the critical item or operation using the benchmark.

7. *Cause-and-effect (fishbone or Ishikawa) diagram* is a tool for analyzing causative factors into layers of categories.

2.4 Statistical Quality Control

Statistical quality control refers to a set of techniques for collecting and analyzing data related to quality performance with the objective of identifying opportunities for quality improvement. Quality control and quality improvement are complementary: applying procedures to achieve control of quality may help identify areas that need quality improvements, and implementation of quality improvement ideas may help identify areas where control is needed.

Traditionally, quality control procedures have been divided into two categories: acceptance sampling and statistical process control. Monitoring of quality is done at three stages of production: input, process, and output. Monitoring done before and after production (input and output) involves acceptance sampling; monitoring during the production process is referred to as process control.

2.5 Acceptance Sampling

Acceptance sampling is used to accept or reject a collection of items, called a lot, based on the inspection of a sample of items taken from the lot. Acceptance sampling is economically advantageous and useful in the following situations, when:

1. A lot with a large number of items is processed in a short period of time.

2. Inspection errors increase as a result of fatigue and boredom caused by an increased workload.

3. The consequences of passing defectives in the process are low.

4. Destructive testing of items is required.

The development of a sampling plan is an important aspect of acceptance sampling. A sampling plan specifies the lot size, sample size, number of samples, and the acceptance/rejection criteria. There are several types of sampling plans:

1. A *single-sampling plan* involves drawing a random sample from each lot and inspecting every item in the sample to find defectives. A lot is rejected if a sample drawn from the lot contains more than a specified number of defectives.

2. A *double-sampling plan* involves the use of two random samples drawn from each lot. It specifies the lot size, size of the first sample, and acceptance/rejection criteria (a range). If the number of defectives is greater than the upper limit of the range, a second sample is used to determine acceptability of the lot.

3. A *multiple-sampling plan* (sequential-sampling) is similar to the double sampling plan—it specifies two limits for each sample. If the number of defects in a sample is greater than the upper limit, new samples are examined. This process continues until a lot is accepted or rejected.

An *Operating Characteristic (OC) curve* is a graphical display of the performance of a sampling plan. It shows the probability that use of the sampling plan will result in lots with various fractions of defective products being accepted. As lot quality decreases, the probability of accepting the lot decreases. Lots with a low percent of defectives have some chance of being rejected, and lots with a very high percent of defectives stand a chance of getting accepted. The steepness of the OC curve indicates how well the sampling plan discriminates between good and bad lots.

The *design of a sampling plan* is based on the following:

a. *Acceptable Quality Level (AQL)* is the quality level acceptable to the customer and is generally stated in the contracts or purchase orders.

b. *Producer's risk (α)* is the probability of rejecting a lot with AQL quality.

c. *Lot Tolerance Proportion Defective (LTPD)* is the worst level of quality that the customer will accept.

d. *Consumer's risk (β)* is the probability of accepting a lot with LTPD quality.

2.6 Statistical Process Control

Statistical process control focuses on monitoring quality during the production process. It involves taking a random sample from a lot and measuring the quality. If the sample measurements are outside a specified range, defined by upper and lower control limits, investigation of the process is done to find the cause of the variation in quality. There is some natural variation in the quality levels between units in the same lot; setting the control limits helps distinguish between normal and abnormal variation.

Some frequently used statistical process control charts are as follows:

1. A *p-chart* is a control chart for attributes, such as number of defects and complaints. A random sample of items is taken, and each item is inspected to find the number of defectives in the sample. The proportion of the sample found to be defective is plotted on a chart and compared against the upper and lower control limits. The *Upper Control Limit (UCL)* and the *Lower Control Limit (LCL)* are calculated using the following equations:

$$UCL = \bar{p} + z\sqrt{\frac{\bar{p}(1 - \bar{p})}{n}} \qquad LCL = \bar{p} - z\sqrt{\frac{\bar{p}(1 - \bar{p})}{n}}$$

where n is the sample size, z is the number of standard deviations from the process average, and $\bar{p}$ is the process average.

$$\bar{p} = \frac{\text{Total number of defects from all samples}}{\text{Number of samples} \times \text{Sample size}}$$

2. *x-charts and R-charts* are control charts used for controlling process average and process variability, respectively. These charts are used for variables that are measured on a continuous scale like weight, length, and time. Random samples are drawn from lots and control limits are developed using sample average, sample range, process average, and process range.

$$\text{Sample average } \bar{x} = \frac{\text{Sum of observations in a sample}}{\text{Number of observations}}$$

$$\text{Sample range } R = \text{Largest } - \text{ Smallest measure in a sample}$$

$$\text{Process average } \bar{\bar{x}} = \frac{\text{Sum of sample averages}}{\text{Number of samples}}$$

$$\text{Process range } \bar{R} = \frac{\text{Sum of sample ranges}}{\text{Number of samples}}$$

The control limits are also based on values of A_2, D_3, and D_4, which provide three standard deviation limits from process average and process range. These values are generally provided in a table in operations management textbooks. The UCL and the LCL for the *x*-chart are calculated using the following equations:

$$UCL = \bar{\bar{x}} + A_2\bar{R} \qquad LCL = \bar{\bar{x}} - A_2\bar{R}$$

The UCL and the LCL for the *R*-chart are calculated using the following equations:

$$UCL = D_4\bar{R} \qquad LCL = D_3\bar{R}$$

11

CHAPTER 3

Forecasting

Forecasting is the basis for most planning activities in all organizations. For instance, in finance it is the basis for building budgets, in marketing it is the basis for planning new products and sales activities, and in operations it is the basis for planning capacity, inventory, and scheduling. A forecast is a statement about the future—an estimate of magnitude, time, or the occurrence of a future event.

Inadequate attention to forecasting leads to poor forecasts, which result in problems such as excessive labor, material, capital costs, and lost customers. Forecasting involves two types of costs: cost of forecasting effort for collecting, maintaining, and analyzing data, and costs as a result of poor forecasts. The objective of forecasting is to find the level of forecasting effort that minimizes the sum of both types of costs. The basic steps involved in forecasting activity are: collection and analysis of data, determination of forecasts, evaluation and determination of forecasts, and control and feedback.

3.1 Types of Forecasting Techniques

Forecasting techniques are classified into four categories:

1. *Qualitative techniques* are subjective and judgmental based on expert judgment and opinions.

2. *Time series analysis* (quantitative) involves using past data to predict future demand.

3. *Causal relationships* describe how demand is related to some factors. The relationship is studied and, given the factors, demand is estimated.

4. *Simulation* involves identifying all factors, building a model that describes the relationship, and then experimenting with the model under different scenarios about the condition of the forecast.

3.2 Components of Demand

The basic components of demand shown in forecasting are:

1. *Average demand*—sum of all demand figures divided by the number of periods.

2. *Seasonality*—similar variations during corresponding periods.

3. *Trend*—gradual long-term directional movement in the data.

4. *Cyclical pattern*—long-term swings about the trend line.

5. *Random data*—sporadic and unpredictable due to chance and unusual occurrences.

3.3 Time Series Techniques

A *simple moving average* involves averaging data over the immediate past and using the average as a forecast. A three-period moving average is obtained by summing the demand figures for the previous three periods and dividing by three. For each period, the oldest figure is dropped from the total and the latest is added to continuously update the forecast. The advantage of this method is that it is easy to understand. A disadvantage with this method is that it gives equal weight to the oldest and the latest demand figures in computing the forecast.

$$F_t = \frac{\sum\limits_{i=t-n}^{t-1} d_i}{n}$$

where F_t is the forecast for the time period t, n is the number of periods used in the moving average, and d_i is the demand in the ith period.

A *weighted moving average* allows some important values to be emphasized by varying the weights assigned to each component of the average. It is computed using the formula:

$$F_t = \sum\limits_{i=t-n}^{t-1} d_i w_i$$

$$\sum\limits_{i=t-n}^{t-1} w_i = 1$$

where w_i is the weight given to demand in period i.

A simple *exponential smoothing* model provides a forecast, F_t, by adding a portion of the error in the prior period to the old forecast from the prior period.

$$F_t = F_{t-1} + \alpha(A_{t-1} - F_{t-1})$$

where α is called the smoothing constant and takes a value between 0 and 1. F_{t-1} and A_{t-1} are the forecast and actual figures from the prior period $(t-1)$.

3.4   Measuring Forecast Accuracy

Controlling the forecast involves monitoring the forecast errors, determining if they are within reasonable bounds, and taking corrective action if they are out of the bounds. *Forecast error* is the difference between actual value (A_t) and forecast (F_t).

$$\text{Error} = (A_t - F_t)$$

14

An important measure for forecast accuracy is the *Mean Absolute Deviation (MAD)*.

$$MAD = \frac{\sum_{i=1}^{n}|A_i - F_i|}{n}$$

Tracking Signal (TS) is a measure that helps monitor forecasts. It is the ratio of the cumulative forecast error to the corresponding value of MAD.

$$\text{Tracking signal} = \frac{\sum_{i=1}^{n}A_i - F_i}{MAD}$$

CHAPTER 4

Product/Service Design

Product design refers to the creation of a model of the product. It is an important factor in customer satisfaction, product quality, and labor and equipment costs. Well-designed products are more likely to help an organization achieve its goals than poorly designed products. The objectives of product design are to:

1. Introduce new or improved products to the market as quickly as possible.

2. Increase the quality and customer-satisfaction levels.

3. Reduce the production costs.

4. Satisfy regulatory requirements.

4.1 Steps in Product Design

The product design activity starts with a motivation for designing the product. The ideas for the new or revised designs come from:

1. Customer information obtained by the marketing department through surveys, focus groups, etc.

2. Competitors, by studying the competitors' products.

3. Internal sources, such as the research and development department.

In general, the marketing, design, and production departments work closely with each other, keeping each other informed, and taking into account the needs and wants of the customer, as well as production capabilities.

Computer Aided Design (CAD) uses computer-based graphics software to design products. CAD refers to the application of computer technology to automate the design process, including geometric modeling, stress and strain analysis, drafting, storing specifications, and allowing simulation of a mechanism's parts. The objectives of CAD include:

1. Improving design productivity.

2. Reducing design lead-time.

3. Improving design quality.

4. Improving access to and storage of product designs.

5. Increasing capability to design a variety of products.

Quality Function Deployment (QFD) is an approach for integrating the "voice of the customer" into the design specifications of the product. This approach uses a tool called the *House of Quality Matrix* that helps organize information about customer requirements and their degree of importance, technical characteristics, their weight and target values, and any competitive information. This matrix helps focus on designing a product that satisfies customers.

4.2 Product Life Cycle

The product life cycle shows how demand for the product changes over time. This pattern varies from product to product. The product life cycle can be divided into the following stages:

1. *Incubation* (introduction)—demand is low due to factors such as less awareness about the product and higher prices.

2. *Growth*—demand increases as a result of higher reliability (if any initial defects are eliminated) and lower prices.

3. *Maturity*—growth slows and demand starts to level off.

4. *Saturation*—no further increase in demand growth.

5. *Decline*—demand for the product declines.

4.3 Reliability

Reliability refers to a measure of the ability of a product to perform its intended function under normal operating conditions. *Normal operating conditions* refer to a set of conditions such as the load, environment, and operating procedures under which a product's reliability is specified. Reliability is expressed as a probability with a value between 0 and 1. A reliability of 0.8 indicates that the probability the product will perform its intended function is 80 percent and that the probability it will not perform is 20 percent. Therefore, it may be expected that out of 100 trials, there would be 20 failures.

An operations manager is concerned with achieving a balance between the potential benefits of improvements to reliability of a product or process and the cost of implementing the improvement programs. The optimal level of reliability is reached when the incremental benefit equals the incremental costs involved. Reliability may be improved by:

1. Improving product design and production techniques.

2. Testing and conducting preventive maintenance.

3. Using backup procedures and tools.

4. Providing training.

System reliability is a function of the reliability of the components and how they are related. The two basic types of arrangements of components are series and parallel. A *parallel arrangement* is generally used for including backup components so that if a component breaks down, the backup component can perform the function. If two components are arranged in parallel (with reliability of r_1 and r_2), the system reliability R is calculated as follows:

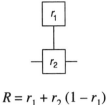

$$R = r_1 + r_2 (1 - r_1)$$

If the components are arranged in a serial manner, the system reliability R is calculated as follows:

$$R = r_1 \times r_2$$

MTBF (Mean Time Between Failures) is the average time between failures for a product and is expressed by a negative exponential distribution. It can be used to determine the probability (P) that a product working from time 0 will fail before a specified time T.

$$P = 1 - e^{\frac{-T}{MTBF}}$$

CHAPTER 5

Process Selection

Process selection refers to the way in which a product is created. Process selection decisions are made when new products are modified or the type of processing is changed. Process selection is based on forecasts of demand and product design. It impacts other operational decisions involving capacity, layout of equipment, design of work, etc.

5.1   Types of Processes

Manufacturing processes are classified into four major categories of operations:

1. *Job shop* produces a wide variety of products, but in small lots, as small as one unit. Due to the wide variety, the processing requirements vary from job to job. In this operation, unit costs and flexibility tend to be high.

2. *Batch production* produces a variety of products in larger lots. It may be considered as a standardized job shop where each type of product follows the same flow pattern through the plant. A food processing factory may produce batches of cans with beans, carrots, and corn. All products may follow similar processes of washing, slicing, cooking, and packaging.

3. *Assembly line operation* produces large volumes of standardized output. The products are produced in discrete units. The variety of products is low; production processes are standardized; unit costs are low; flexibility is low; and machine utilization is high.

4. *Continuous processing* also produces large volumes of standardized output, but the products are measured on a continuous basis. Examples of products produced in this operation are oil and liquid chemicals.

Service operations processes are generally classified based on the level of customer contact.

1. *High contact*—In this type of process, the customer spends a large percentage of time in the operation relative to the total time it takes for the overall service. Production efficiency is low, since the customer can significantly affect the operation. Examples of this type of operation are legal and medical services.

2. *Low contact*—Customers spend little or no time in the operation relative to the total time for the service. In the case of a mail-order operation, there is no interaction (or little interaction if contacted by phone) with the customer. Hence, the production efficiency is high in this type of process.

A *product-process matrix* shows the relationship between products and types of processes. Products and processes are shown on two sides of the matrix: the process side of the matrix shows the type of process from job shop to continuous process; and the product side of the matrix shows the product life cycle of the firm with output ranging from a low-volume, one-of-a-kind product to a high-volume standardized product. Organizations are often points on the diagonal of the matrix.

5.2 Selecting Equipment

Process type indicates the equipment suitable for production: a job shop requires general purpose machines to produce a variety of products, whereas an assembly operation requires special purpose dedicated machines to produce large quantities efficiently. Several factors are considered in the selection of equipment. These include price, ease of use, output rate and quality, availability of parts, and skills and training requirements. A commonly used approach for selecting equipment is break-even analysis, which considers initial investment, variable costs incurred in operating the equipment, and anticipated demand.

Equipment selection decisions are made when adding resources to existing operations or replacing existing resources. The type of equipment that is capable of producing at the lowest cost to meet the anticipated demand is the preferred alternative if the focus is on economic criterion. Break-even analysis provides "break points" which help in the selection of the best equipment.

Total cost = Fixed cost + Variable cost × Anticipated demand

Given the initial investment (fixed cost) and the variable cost of producing each unit for all the alternatives, the above equation can be used to calculate total cost for each alternative over a range of production volumes. The alternative which results in the least cost for a specified range of anticipated demand is selected.

5.3 Design of Processes

Design of manufacturing and service processes involves identifying all the steps involved in creating a product or delivering a service. The basic tools used in designing manufacturing processes include:

1. *Assembly drawings*—show all the component parts of the product.

2. *Assembly charts*—use information in the assembly drawings and list all the parts and how they are assembled.

3. *Operation and route sheets*—show the operation and process routing for a specific part.

4. *Process flow charts*—list all the steps that transform inputs to outputs and show the flow of materials and storage.

CHAPTER 6

Just-in-Time Production System

Just-in-Time (JIT) refers to a repetitive production system in which all activities are carefully timed so that materials and parts arrive at a particular stage of production only when they are needed. The JIT approach was developed at the Toyota Motor Company in Japan. JIT can be considered a "philosophy" that encompasses all aspects of production from product design to after-sale service. However, JIT is generally considered a system for repetitive production which provides many benefits.

6.1 Benefits of a JIT System

Many U.S. manufacturing firms are implementing JIT systems to realize benefits such as:

1. Reduced inventory levels.

2. Reduced manufacturing lead times.

3. Encouragement of worker participation in problem solving.

4. Improved relationships with suppliers.

5. Smooth production flow by removing disruptions and inefficiency and improving product quality.

6.2 Characteristics of a JIT System

JIT systems display certain unique characteristics that help achieve a smooth flow of production and benefits. Key characteristics of the JIT system include:

1. *Pull system*—Purchase of the final product by the customer *pulls* output from the final stage of production, which in turn *pulls* output from the preceding stages of production. Each production stage *pulls* output from the preceding stages when it is needed. Hence, a JIT system is considered a *pull* system.

2. *Quality*—JIT systems require high-quality levels for product design, production process, and raw materials/parts supplied by the vendors. Also, workers are provided with adequate tools, training, support, encouragement, and authority for ensuring production of high-quality goods.

3. *Small lot sizes*—JIT systems use small lot sizes in the production process and therefore require small deliveries from suppliers. Small lot sizes permit greater flexibility in scheduling and reduce in-process inventory. Flexibility enables quick response to changing customer demands. Reduced inventory levels help minimize holding costs, space, and clutter. Also, smaller lots require less inspection and lower rework costs.

4. *Quick setups*—Setup procedures are simple and standardized to enable frequent and quick setups required due to smaller lot sizes.

5. *Production smoothing*—To ensure a smooth flow of goods from the supplier to the final stage of production, all activities are carefully coordinated and changes to the production plan are minimized.

6. *Suppliers*—Since the JIT system requires high-quality materials delivered on-time and uses small lot sizes, it also requires reliable suppliers who are willing to ship high-quality materials and parts on a regular basis.

7. *Kanban card*—Communication between a production stage and the preceding stages is carried out in various ways to ensure timely and smooth movement of parts and materials. The Kanban card is a commonly used tool (e.g., at Toyota) for communicating the need for parts or work from a preceding production stage. Without this card, which serves as an authorization, no part or lot can be moved.

EXAMPLE

In the following two-card kanban system, the machine center supplies part P to the assembly line. Withdrawal and production kanbans are used to authorize production and transfer of part P to the assembly line for final processing.

When a part P has been incorporated into the finished product at the assembly line, a withdrawal kanban is taken from the assembly line to a storage area where it is exchanged for a new part P. At that time, a production kanban is delivered from the storage area to the machine center, thus authorizing production of a new part P. The new part is then brought to the storage area where it waits to be exchanged for another withdrawal kanban when needed at the assembly line.

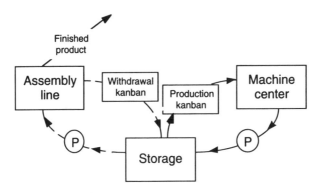

6.3 Comparison Between JIT and Traditional Systems

The JIT approach is fundamentally different from the traditional manufacturing philosophy. The following is a summary of the important differences between JIT and traditional manufacturing systems:

	JIT	**Traditional**
Movement of work	Pull system	Push system
Quality	Zero defects	Tolerate some scrap
Lot sizes	Small	Based on trade-off between inventory and setup costs
Setups	Quick and frequent	Not an important factor
Inventory	A liability—should be removed	An asset—used for protection

CHAPTER 7

Capacity Planning

Capacity planning deals with specifying the capacity level of resources such as workforce level, equipment, and facilities to support the organization's production strategy. Capacity planning decisions are classified into three main categories based on time durations:

1. *Long term*—relating to overall capacity such as facility size, acquisition or disposal of equipment, buildings, and facilities.

2. *Medium term*—relating to setting workforce levels and subcontracting.

3. *Short term*—relating to production schedules, overtime, etc.

Capacity may be defined as an upper limit on the load that an operating unit can handle, and in a general sense, it can be defined as the capability of an organization to produce some quantity of output in a specific time period.

Capacity planning is important for the following reasons: capacity indicates the ability of the organization to meet future demands for products or services; operating costs can be reduced if capacity is matched with demand; and planning involves long-term commitment of resources. Capacity planning involves: measuring capacity, determining capacity requirements, and evaluating capacity alternatives.

7.1 Capacity Concepts

Economies of scale means that if the size of a facility is increased (if capacity is increased), the average unit cost decreases. The unit cost decreases as the facility becomes more efficient. This occurs when the facility becomes large enough to fully utilize dedicated resources and has the ability to distribute nondirect (i.e., fixed) costs, such as research and development, and administrative costs over a large number of units. However, after a facility reaches a certain limit, *diseconomies of scale* set in, since the excessive size brings in complexities, inefficiencies, and loss of focus.

A *learning curve* refers to the relationship between unit production time, or cost, and the number of consecutive units produced. It deals with improvements resulting from repeating a process and gaining efficiency. Individual learning results from repetition and instruction; organizational learning results from gaining experience in product and process design, automation, changes in administrative methods, etc. Learning curves enable operations managers to estimate the unit production cost for a given level of output.

Assuming that production time (or cost) per unit is reduced by a fixed percentage each time the production is doubled, the learning curve can be expressed as

$$k_n = k_1 n^{\frac{\log r}{\log 2}}$$

where k_n is the production time required for the nth unit, k_1 is the production time required for the first unit, and r is the learning rate. For example, assuming an 80% learning rate and 50 minutes to produce the first unit, the time required to produce the 40th unit is $50 \times 40^{\log .80/\log 2} = 15.25$ minutes.

7.2 Capacity Measures

Capacity may be expressed in terms of inputs (number of beds for a hospital or number of square feet for a department store) or outputs (number of automobiles per year for an auto manufacturer or tons of steel per year for a steel plant) to quantify production capacity.

28

Design capacity (or *theoretical capacity*) is the maximum output that can be achieved. *Demonstrated capacity* (or *actual output*) is the output actually achieved. This is less than the design capacity due to changes in the product mix, maintenance of equipment, scheduling problems, defective output, and shortages of materials. The *best operating level*, another measure for expressing capacity, is the level of capacity for which the process is designed. It refers to a volume of output that results in the minimum average unit cost.

Capacity utilization is the ratio of actual output to design capacity and is expressed as a percentage (both capacity measures should be expressed in the same terms). Capacity utilization is an indicator of the need for adding extra capacity. *Capacity cushion* is the amount by which the average utilization rate falls below 100% (capacity cushion = 100 − average utilization rate).

7.3 Determining Capacity Requirements

Capacity requirements are determined using information about demand for individual products and the production capabilities of the firm. The basic steps involved in this process are:

1. Obtain forecasts of sales for individual products from marketing.

2. Compute equipment and labor requirements to meet forecasts.

3. Project labor and equipment availability over the planning horizon.

7.4 Evaluating Capacity Alternatives

To achieve desired capacity levels, a variety of capacity alternatives may be considered (for example, capacity levels may be increased or decreased). When developing capacity alternatives, it is important to consider:

1. Increasing capacity in small or large increments.

2. Maintaining system balance by adding capacity to bottleneck operations.

3. Using subcontracting, inventories, and overtime.

Capacity alternatives must be examined from various perspectives in the evaluation process, such as:

1. Economic considerations—costs and time.

2. Impact on workforce—terminating or retraining employees and morale issues.

3. Relationship with community—if capacity increase impacts noise and pollution levels.

Evaluation of capacity alternatives can be accomplished with financial analysis, simulation or queuing analysis, or decision analysis.

Break-even analysis is a commonly used financial analysis tool which deals with the relationship between cost, revenues, and volume of output. An important result of this analysis is the break-even quantity, which is expressed as:

$$\text{Break-even quantity} = \frac{\text{Fixed cost}}{(\text{Revenue per unit} - \text{Unit cost})}$$

A break-even quantity level for each alternative helps a manager to rank the alternatives and select the best capacity alternative.

A *decision tree* is a commonly used decision analysis tool. It is a schematic model composed of nodes representing multiphase decision points and chance events, as well as branches showing the probabilities of occurrence of the chance events. Generally, branches from the first decision node in the tree are used to represent the main capacity alternatives. The last branches in the tree have payoffs associated with them. The solution procedure involves working backwards (from the last decision to the beginning) by multiplying the payoffs with the probabilities to get expected payoffs. The alternative with the greatest expected payoff is selected.

CHAPTER 8

Facility Location

Choosing facility locations involves planning and analysis to determine which locations offer the best profit potential (for profit-oriented organizations), or a balance between cost and level of customer service (for nonprofit-oriented organizations). Location planning is an integral part of the strategic planning process and has a significant impact on the organization. Establishing a facility involves a long-term commitment. Over time, location-related variables can have a significant impact on operating costs and revenues.

Establishing a facility in a poor location may result in increased transportation costs, shortage of qualified labor, loss of competitive advantage, inadequate supplies of raw materials, and loss of customers.

8.1 Reasons for Locating Facilities

Organizations become involved in locational decisions for a variety of reasons, such as:

1. Part of marketing strategy—organizations seek to establish facilities in locations that will expand their markets (banks, fast-food restaurants, retail stores).

2. Existing location cannot satisfy growth in demand—addition of a new location may be needed to complement the existing system (manufacturing).

31

3. Depletion of natural resources at existing locations (fishing, logging, mining, oil).

4. Shift in markets causes organizations to relocate (relocating regional construction offices to new construction sites).

5. Costs of doing business at a particular location reach a point where other locations look attractive (moving production facilities to Mexico, Asia, etc.).

8.2 Factors that Affect Location Decisions

Factors affecting location decisions include:

1. Proximity to customers and source of raw materials due to: necessity—mining, fishing, and farming; perishability—firms involved in canning and freezing fruit and vegetables; and transportation—to reduce transport costs.

2. Infrastructure, including energy, telecommunications, and transportation, is vital. The willingness of the government to upgrade the infrastructure is also important.

3. Availability of labor and the host community's interest in having the facility in its midst.

8.3 Procedure for Selecting a Location

The general procedure for making location decisions involves the following steps:

1. Decide criteria (increased revenue, customer service).

2. Identify important factors (location of markets, raw materials).

3. Develop alternatives, identify a general region for location, and identify community site alternatives.

4. Evaluate alternatives and make a selection.

Evaluation of alternative regions and communities is commonly called macroanalysis, and the evaluation of specific sites in the selected community is called microanalysis. There are various procedures for analysis, including factor-rating procedures, linear programming, center-of-gravity method, and locational cost-volume analysis.

8.3.1 Factor-rating method

The *factor-rating method* is widely used and easy to understand. It helps organize and combine both quantitative and qualitative factors in the decision process. The steps are:

1. Develop a list of locations and relevant factors.

2. Assign a weight for each factor.

3. Assign a score for each alternative.

4. Multiply the score and weight.

5. Sum the weighted scores for each location.

6. Select the location that has the highest score.

In the example below, Location B is preferred because it has the highest score based on the factors, their weights, and the scores for each location.

Relevant Factors	Weight	Location A		Location B	
		Score	Weighted Score	Score	Weighted Score
Production cost	0.5	80	$0.5 \times 80 = 40$	60	$0.5 \times 60 = 30$
Availability of labor	0.3	40	$0.3 \times 40 = 12$	80	$0.3 \times 80 = 24$
Markets	0.1	60	$0.1 \times 60 = 6$	50	$0.1 \times 50 = 5$
Environment	0.1	20	$0.1 \times 20 = 2$	60	$0.1 \times 60 = 6$
Total	**1.0**		**60**		**65**

8.3.2 Linear programming

This method involves the formulation of a mathematical model which incorporates factors related to the facility location problem.

33

Typically, variables in the model take a value of 1 or 0, indicating the selection or elimination of a potential site. The objective functions in the linear programming model may seek to maximize potential customers or revenue, minimize distance and costs, and minimize customer response times. This approach is suitable for complex facility location problems with several alternatives and selection criteria.

The following model has the objective function of minimizing total transportation costs; constants specify supply limitations and demand requirements.

$$\text{Min } z(x) = \sum_{i=1}^{m} \sum_{j=1}^{n} c_{ij} x_{ij}$$

subject to

$$\sum_{j=1}^{n} x_{ij} = a_i, i = 1, 2, \ldots, m$$

$$\sum_{i=1}^{m} x_{ij} = b_j, j = 1, 2, \ldots, n$$

$x_{ij} \geq 0$ for all i and j

where c_{ij} represents the cost of transporting one unit of a common product from source i to destination j. The constants a_i and b_j represent the supply limitation at source i and the demand requirement at destination j, respectively. X_{ij} represents the amount transported from location i to location j.

8.3.3   Center-of-gravity method

The *center-of-gravity method* can be used to locate a single facility by considering existing facilities, distances between them, and volumes of goods shipped between them. The first step in this method is to place existing locations on a coordinate grid system. Using relative distances, the following formulas give the x and y coordinates for the new facility, which results in the least transportation cost.

$$C_x = \frac{\sum_i d_{ix} V_i}{\sum_i V_i} \qquad C_y = \frac{\sum_i d_{iy} V_i}{\sum_i V_i}$$

where (C_x, C_y) are the x and y coordinates of the new facility, (d_{ix}, d_{iy}) are the x and y coordinates of the ith facility, and V_i is the volume of goods for the ith facility.

8.3.4 Locational cost-volume analysis

This method is useful for evaluating location alternatives based on economic criteria. First, revenues and fixed and variable costs associated with each location alternative are estimated. Second, expected profit for each location is determined for a specified range of production levels. Finally, a location that offers the maximum expected profit or minimum total costs for producing the desired level of production is selected.

CHAPTER 9

Facility Layout

Facility layout refers to the configuration or arrangement of departments, machines, and workcenters in a facility (departments in a hospital or machines in a manufacturing plant). Facility layout decisions are important because:

1. They require substantial investment of money and effort.
2. They involve long-term commitment—mistakes are difficult to correct.
3. They have significant impact on cost and productivity of short-term operations.
4. Personnel may resist changes to an existing or proposed layout because it alters daily routines and may require retraining.

The primary objectives of facility layout planning are:

1. Minimizing the cost of moving material through the system.
2. Minimizing the cost of moving customers through the system.
3. Minimizing the number of customers waiting in the line and the amount of time spent in the line.
4. Maximizing customer satisfaction.
5. Improving the quality of the product or service.
6. Maximizing productivity.

The need for layout arises when new facilities are established.

Also, layout planning is required when old facilities are redesigned for:

1. Producing new products.
2. Producing a new mix of products.
3. Improving operations that have bottlenecks or high costs.
4. Addressing changes in methods of equipment.

9.1 Types of Layouts

There are three basic types of facility layouts:

1. *Process layout*—Departments are arranged in such a way that each department performs the same types of activities or processes.
2. *Product layout*—Departments or machines are arranged according to the sequence of tasks required to produce the product. Layout is dedicated to a product line.
3. *Fixed-position layout*—the product remains in the same position and resources (workers, machines, materials) are moved as needed. Nature of the product (weight and size) dictates this type of arrangement.

9.2 Product vs. Process Layout

The main differences between product and process layouts are summarized as follows:

Process Layout	Product Layout
Less machine utilization	High machine utilization
Suited for medium volume production with a variety of products	Suited for high volume production and less variety of products
Fewer spare parts, tools	More spare parts, tools
Low vulnerability to production shutdown	High vulnerability to production shutdown

9.3   Design Techniques

There are different techniques for designing the process and product layouts.

9.3.1 Process layout

A common objective in designing a process layout is to arrange workcenters that have high interaction closer to each other so as to minimize the flow of material. This procedure includes the following steps:

1. Determine the number of departments and the number of links with other departments.

2. Locate the most active departments in central positions.

3. Use a trial-and-error method to locate other departments so that the flow between nonadjacent departments is minimized. Flow between departments A and B = Number of units moving between A and B multiplied by the distance between A and B.

Popular techniques for designing a process layout are CRAFT and SLP techniques. *CRAFT (Computerized Relative Allocation of Facilities Technique)* involves the use of quantitative information about distances between departments, number of movements between departments, and cost per unit distance traveled. Using this information, CRAFT tries to improve the relative placement of the departments by exchanging pairs of departments in an iterative manner until no further cost reductions are possible. The output from the program includes a plotted floor planblock layout and cost of the layout.

SLP (Systematic Layout Planning) technique is used for designing a process layout when quantitative information is not available. It is based on specification of a code indicating the degree of importance for having two departments close to each other. The code is then converted into numerical weights that are used in evaluating different layout arrangements. These weights are determined in an ad-hoc manner, but the logic involves assigning a large weight to indicate desirability of proximity between departments and a small weight to indicate departments need not be close to each other.

Weight	Code	Degree of Importance
16	A	Absolutely Necessary
8	E	Very Important
4	I	Important
2	O	OK, Ordinary Importance
0	U	Unimportant
–80	X	Undesirable

9.3.2 Product layout

A product layout is designed using the *assembly-line balancing* method. This method involves assigning all tasks to a series of workstations so that each workstation has no more than the cycle time, and the idle time across all workstations is minimized. The steps in this method include:

1. List all the tasks in a sequence.

2. Determine cycle time and the minimum number of machines needed to satisfy the cycle time.

$$\text{Cycle Time } (CT) = \frac{\text{Available time per day}}{\text{Output desired per day}}$$

$$\text{Number of machines } (N) = \frac{\text{Sum of task times } (T)}{\text{Cycle Time } (CT)}$$

3. Assign tasks to machines using a decision rule.

4. Evaluate efficiency of the balance.

$$\text{Efficiency } (E) = \frac{\text{Sum of task times } (T)}{\text{Actual number of machines } (N) \times \text{Cycle Time } (CT)}$$

An efficient balance will minimize the idle time (I).

$$I = CT \times N - \text{Sum of task} \times T$$

5. If the efficiency is unsatisfactory, repeat step 3.

CHAPTER 10

Design of Work Systems

Design of work systems involves two major activities—job design and work measurement. *Job design* deals with structuring the work activities of an individual or work group within an organizational setting with the objective of maximizing productivity and efficiency while satisfying the needs of the worker or work group. *Work measurement methods* are used to set standards for performing a task and for determining the most efficient way of performing a task.

10.1 Job Design

Design of jobs involves consideration of behavioral and economic criteria. Behavioral approaches involve job enrichment, job rotation, and job enlargement to make jobs more interesting and meaningful.

Job enrichment refers to an increase in the level of responsibility for planning and coordinating tasks so as to improve worker satisfaction. *Job rotation* refers to workers exchanging jobs. This reduces boredom, allows workers to broaden their skills and learning experience, and enables workers to fill in for absent workers. *Job enlargement* refers to assigning a larger portion of the total task to the worker. This provides the worker with a more recognizable contribution to the overall output.

The *economic approaches* to job design focus on the benefits of specialization of labor, which refers to concentration on a specific task. Specialization of labor offers various benefits to the organization, such as higher productivity, lower wages, and training costs; and offers labor such benefits as low skill requirements and minimal responsibilities. However, there are disadvantages, such as worker dissatisfaction, poor attention to quality, monotonous boring work, and limited opportunities for career advancement.

10.2 Work Measurement

Work measurement methods are used for setting time standards for the following reasons:

1. To help schedule operations.

2. To help capacity planning.

3. To evaluate performance and motivate workforce.

4. To bid for contracts and establish prices and costs.

5. To provide benchmarks for improvements.

10.3 Work Measurement Techniques

There are four basic techniques for measuring work:

1. *Time study*—Work is divided into measurable parts and each part is timed by using a stop watch on the spot or by analyzing a video recording of the work. A time standard is developed based on observations taken over a number of cycles. The steps involved in this method are:

   a. Define the task to be studied.

   b. Determine the number of cycles to be studied.

   c. Find the time for the job.

   d. Rate the performance of workers.

   e. Calculate the standard time.

The number of cycles that must be observed is based on desired accuracy, variability of observed times, and desired level of confidence for the estimated job time.

Observed time for a task is the average of all the observed times. *Normal time* is the observed time adjusted for worker performance by multiplying with a performance rating. *Standard time* is the normal time adjusted for certain delays (such as personal delays, breaks, and machine breakdowns) by multiplying with an allowance factor.

The advantages of the time study method are that it helps set reasonable standards and it is easy to understand. The disadvantages are that it is not suitable for jobs that change each time they are performed, and unions may object to time study because of the judgment and subjectivity involved.

2. *Elemental standard time data*—Data within tables or company databases from previous time studies are used to develop time standards for new jobs. This procedure includes the following steps:

   a. Divide the job into basic tasks/elements.

   b. Check if these elements are available in historical files. For those without historical times, conduct a time study.

   c. Adjust times if necessary.

   d. Add all the elemental times to obtain the normal time and adjust it to allow for delays and fatigue to obtain the standard time.

   Advantages of this procedure are reduced cost and time (since a complete time study is not required) and less disruption of work. Disadvantages are that historical times may be biased or inaccurate, and times may not be available for enough elements to make this procedure economical.

3. *Predetermined Motion-Time Data Systems* (*PMTS*)—Existing published data, such as Motion-Time-Measurement (MTM) tables, are used to develop time standards. While

elemental standard time data is company- or industry-specific, PMTS is generic and provides times for basic motions. The times for the basic motions are expressed in TMUs (Time Measurement Units), which are equal to 0.0006 minutes. This procedure may be considered an extension of the previous approach. The basic steps involved in this procedure are:

a. Divide each work element into a series of micro-motions, such as reach, move, grasp, position, release, etc.

b. Obtain normal times for the micro-motions from MTM databases.

c. Rate the degree of difficulty for each motion.

d. Add normal times for each motion to obtain a normal time for the task.

e. Adjust the normal time for allowances to obtain standard times.

The advantages of this method are that there is no disruption to the operation; standards can be established before the production begins; and performance ratings are not needed to derive the standards. Disadvantages are that considerable skills and expertise are needed to conduct the study, and it may be impractical for non-repetitive jobs.

4. *Work-sampling* involves estimating the proportion of time a worker spends on various activities, such as producing a product and waiting for instructions. These estimates are based on a large number of observations. The assumption is that the proportion of time the activity is observed in the sample will be the proportion of time spent on the activity. The advantages of the work-sampling method are that no timing devices are needed; multiple studies can be conducted simultaneously; and studies are economical and no special skills are required. The disadvantages are that it is based on a large number of observations; it provides less detail on the elements of a job; and it is not suited for short repetitive jobs.

CHAPTER 11

Project Management

Project management is the planning, scheduling, and control of resources to accomplish a specific set of objectives while meeting the time, cost, and technical constraints of a project. A project is a set of activities that is completed in a particular sequence and has definite beginning and ending points. All project management decisions involve three factors: time, cost, and resources such as manpower and equipment.

Project management is carried out in three stages:

1. *Project planning*, which deals with defining project activities and sequence, determining the resource needs for each project activity, and specifying the performance criteria.

2. *Project scheduling*, which deals with determining when the project activities will be performed. This enables the manager to assign resources effectively.

3. *Project control*, which deals with checking the status of the project activities, comparing them with the plan, and initiating corrective action to ensure that the project is completed on schedule (within time, cost, and quality targets).

11.1 Basic Steps

Typically, all projects involve the following steps:

1. Describe the project.
2. Develop a network model.
3. Specify time and cost estimates.
4. Analyze the model.
5. Develop a project plan.
6. Monitor and control the project.

11.2 Activity Times

To overcome the uncertainty inherent in times, a commonly used method involves computing an expected time for an activity using three time estimates:

1. *Most optimistic time (a)*—shortest time in which an activity can be completed, if everything progresses in an ideal manner.

2. *Most likely time (m)*—best estimate of time required to perform an activity under normal conditions.

3. *Most pessimistic time (b)*—longest estimated time required to perform an activity, assuming that significant delays are encountered.

Using the beta distribution, Expected Time (ET) and variance (σ^2) of the activity times can be calculated as follows:

$$ET = \frac{a + 4m + b}{6}$$

$$\sigma^2 = \left(\frac{b - a}{6}\right)^2$$

The difference between the pessimistic time and optimistic time greatly affects the variance of an activity.

11.3   Network Models

A network model consists of nodes/circles and arcs/arrows that denote the project activities and their relationship. There are two methods for modeling networks: *A-O-A* (Activity-on-Arrow) network, which uses arrows to represent activities and nodes to represent events (such as the start and end of an activity) and *A-O-N* (Activity-on-Node) network, which uses nodes to represent activities and arrows to represent the sequence or relationship between activities.

Network models are the basis for two widely used methods developed in the 1950s: CPM—Critical Path Method, and PERT—Program Evaluation and Review Technique. In the past, CPM used deterministic single-time estimates, whereas PERT employed multiple probabilistic time estimates. CPM and PERT, which were significantly different in the past, are no longer differentiated and are generally referred to as CPM/PERT.

11.3.1 Advantages of CPM/PERT

CPM/PERT offers several benefits in project management. These methods:

1. Provide a graphical display of project activities.

2. Provide an estimate of the project completion time.

3. Indicate activities that are critical for timely completion of the project.

4. Indicate how long an activity can be delayed without delaying the project.

5. Help a manager to organize and quantify information.

11.4   Project Scheduling

A sequence of activities in a network model from the start to the end is called a *path*. *Path time* is the sum of times of all the activities on the path. A *critical path* is a path with the longest time sequence. Activities on this path are considered to be critical for completion of the project. The project gets delayed if any activity on the critical path is delayed.

Project completion time is equal to the sum of times required by activities on the critical path. *Path slack* is the difference between the critical path time and time for the given path. *Activity slack* is the maximum amount of time an activity can be delayed without delaying the project. It is computed using time information related to each activity, including:

1. *ES (Earliest Start time)* is the earliest possible beginning time for an activity.

2. *LS (Latest Start time)* is the latest possible beginning time for an activity that will allow the project to be completed on schedule.

3. *EF (Earliest Finish time)* is the earliest start time *(ES)* plus the time needed for an activity.

4. *LF (Latest Finish time)* is the latest possible completion time for an activity that will allow the project to be completed on schedule.

Probability of completing a project within a desired time period can be derived if the three probabilistic time estimates are specified for each activity. This probability helps in understanding the effect of uncertainty in time estimates upon completion of the project. The steps in calculating the probability are:

1. Identify the critical path and determine expected project completion time (T).

2. Calculate variance for each activity.

3. Sum the variances associated with each activity on the critical path $\left(\Sigma \sigma cp^2 \right)$.

4. Specify the desired completion time.

5. Use the following equation to find the value of z.

$$z = \frac{D - T}{\sqrt{\Sigma \sigma cp^2}}$$

Refer to the Areas of the Cumulative Standard Normal Distribution table at the end of this book and find the probability associated with the z-value. This refers to the probability of completing the project within the desired completion time D.

11.5 Time-Cost Models

Project completion times can be reduced by using additional resources. *Crashing*, which refers to shortening the project duration, results in reduction of indirect project costs (such as facilities, equipment costs, and supervision costs) and an increase in direct project costs (such as costs for additional direct labor, materials, and better equipment). The objective of using time-cost trade-off models is to identify a plan that will minimize the sum of indirect and direct project costs.

Project completion time can be reduced by making a trade-off between direct and indirect project costs using the following procedure:

1. Develop a network diagram. For each activity in the network identify the normal cost (NC) and normal time (NT), and the crash cost (CC) and crash time (CT). Note that crash cost is higher than the normal cost.

2. Determine the cost per unit of time (days, for example) to expedite each activity by taking the slope of the relationship between the cost and time.

$$\text{Cost per day to expedite} = \frac{CC - NC}{NT - CT}$$

3. Determine the critical path.

4. Shorten the critical path by expediting the activity with the least cost by one day.

5. Determine the new critical path. Perform Step 4 again. Repeat this process until the time of completion is satisfactory or no further reduction in project completion time is possible.

CHAPTER 12

Aggregate Planning

Aggregate planning involves translating annual and quarterly business plans into production plans which specify an optimal combination of production rate, staffing levels, and inventory levels for the intermediate term (2–12 months). The goal of aggregate planning is to achieve a production plan that effectively utilizes resources to satisfy expected demand.

The basic problem addressed by aggregate planning is the balance of capacity and demand. Aggregate planning starts with a forecast of expected demand for the intermediate range and determines the optimum level of production, inventory, and workforce to meet the desired requirements. A number of plans are considered and evaluated based on costs and other factors that may affect feasibility. The result of the aggregate planning process is a feasible production plan that achieves a balance between expected demand and capacity.

12.1   Demand and Capacity Options

To achieve a balance between expected demand and capacity, various options that change demand or capacity are considered. Options that can alter demand include pricing changes, sales promotion, back orders, and generation of new demand. Capacity options include hiring and firing workers, overtime, part-time workers, inventories, and subcontracting.

12.2　Inputs

The aggregate planning process requires the following inputs:

1. Forecast of expected demand.

2. Information about costs—production and inventory, hiring/ firing, subcontracting, overtime, and back orders.

3. Resources—labor, equipment, and facilities.

4. Company policies regarding overtime, hiring, and subcontracting.

12.3　Basic Strategies

The two basic strategies that can be used for aggregate planning are:

Level capacity strategy—maintains a steady rate of output while meeting variation in demand by using inventories, backlogging, and subcontracting. The advantages are reduced costs of hiring and training, less overtime, fewer morale problems, and a stable utilization of the resource. The disadvantages are lost sales, increased record keeping, lower customer service levels, and increased subcontracting costs. Also, using inventories to absorb variation in demand may result in increased inventory costs.

Chase demand strategy—matches expected demand with capacity. Advantages of the chase strategy are low levels of inventories and better customer service; the disadvantages are lack of stability in operations, more morale problems, and increased hiring and training expenses.

12.4　Techniques

The techniques for solving the aggregate planning problem are the trial and error method, linear programming, and simulation.

The basic steps in the aggregate planning process are:

1. Determine demand for each time period.

2. Determine capacity for each time period (regular time, overtime, and subcontracting).

3. Identify relevant policies (service levels, hiring, and overtime policies).

4. Determine unit costs for regular time, overtime, subcontracting, inventory, back orders, and other relevant costs.

5. Develop alternative plans.

6. Compute costs for each plan.

7. Identify plans that meet all constraints and eliminate others.

8. Rank all alternatives based on costs and other relevant criteria.

9. Select the best plan.

12.5   Disaggregating the Aggregate Plan

Disaggregating the aggregate plan involves conversion of the production plan into specific product requirements to determine labor, material, and inventory requirements. Aggregate units are converted into units for actual products and services. The result of this process is the master schedule, which shows quantity and timing of specific end items. The master schedule is used to perform rough-cut capacity planning to ensure that adequate capacity is available to support the master schedule.

CHAPTER 13

Inventory Management

Inventory is the stock of any item or resource held by an organization for future use. *Inventory management* refers to all the activities involved in maintaining the inventory at a level that results in desired levels of customer service and costs.

Manufacturing inventory can be classified into raw materials or purchased parts; finished products; parts, tools, and supplies; and work-in-process inventory. Manufacturers maintain inventory to:

1. Meet anticipated demand.

2. Smooth production requirements.

3. Protect against delay in supply of materials.

4. Hedge against price increases.

5. Take advantage of quantity discounts.

13.1 Types of Demand

Independent demand inventory consists of finished products or other end items whose demand is not dependent on the demand for other products. *Dependent demand inventory* consists of raw materials, components, and sub-assemblies used in the production of parent items or end items. Demand for these items is derived from the demand for end items.

Dependent demand can be calculated using the demand figures for the end items. Due to the uncertainty involved, independent demand is determined using forecasting methods. This chapter focuses on the management of independent demand inventory.

13.2 Basic Requirements

Effective inventory management requires the following:

1. Classification method for inventory items.

2. An inventory accounting system.

3. Reliable demand forecasts.

4. Information about lead times.

5. Estimates of costs (holding, order placement, and shortage costs).

6. Methods for determining quantity and timing of orders.

13.3 ABC Approach

The *ABC approach* is used for classifying inventory items based on some measure of importance, such as annual dollar usage (dollar value per unit multiplied by annual usage rate) and allocating control efforts accordingly. While the number of categories and percentages may vary, typically, the items are grouped into three categories:

A (very important)—accounts for 20% of the number of items in the inventory with about 65% of the dollar usage value.

B (moderately important)—accounts for 30% of the number of items in the inventory with about 25% of the dollar usage value.

C (least important)—accounts for 50% of the items in the inventory with about 10% of the dollar usage value.

The actual percentage may vary from organization to organization. It is commonly found that a small percentage of items accounts for a large percentage of annual cost volume usage. The advantage of the ABC approach is that it helps identify items that will make the largest impact on the firm's inventory performance when improved inventory control procedures are implemented. An item may be critical, regardless of its classification, if its absence results in a significant loss to the organization.

13.4 Inventory Costs

There are three basic types of inventory costs:

1. *Holding or carrying costs* pertain to physically holding items in storage. This category includes warehousing costs (such as heat, light, rent, security), handling, breakage, pilferage, interest, insurance, depreciation, etc. Also included are opportunity costs associated with having funds tied up in inventory. The holding costs are expressed as a percentage of unit price or dollar amount per unit.

2. *Ordering costs* pertain to managerial and clerical costs to prepare an order and receive inventory. These are expressed as a dollar amount per order.

3. *Shortage (stockout) costs* pertain to the result of a shortage in inventory when demand exceeds the supply of inventory on hand. This category includes the opportunity costs of not having a sale, downtime, loss of goodwill, etc.

A measure for checking how effectively inventory is being used is the *inventory turn ratio*:

$$\text{Inventory turn} = \frac{\text{Annual cost of goods sold}}{\text{Average inventory in dollars}}$$

If the annual cost of goods sold is $1,000,000 and the average inventory is $500,000, then the inventory turn ratio = 2. If the annual cost of carrying inventory is 10% of the purchase costs, the annual cost of carrying inventory in the above example is $50,000. The carrying cost can be reduced by lowering the average inventory. Lowering the average inventory increases the inventory turn ratio.

13.5 Fixed Order Quantity Model

This model is used to determine the size of the order (number of units) Q and the reorder point R at which the order will be placed. The reorder point is expressed in terms of the number of units of an item in the inventory. This model may be described as follows: Place an order for Q units when a withdrawal brings the inventory level to the reorder point R, which is the minimum level allowed.

The order quantity at which total holding costs and total order placement costs are at the minimum is called the *Economic Order Quantity (EOQ)*:

$$EOQ = \sqrt{\frac{2DS}{H}}$$

where D is the annual demand, S is the order placement cost, and H is the annual holding cost per unit.

Total holding cost is the average inventory multiplied by annual holding cost per unit $\frac{Q}{2}H$. Holding costs are a linear function of order quantity. They change in direct proportion to a change in the order quantity.

The number of orders placed in a year = $\frac{D}{Q}$. The length of the order cycle expressed as a fraction of a year is $\frac{Q}{D}$.

Total annual order placement costs are the total number of orders placed in a year multiplied by the order placement cost per order $\frac{D}{Q}S$. Order placement costs are inversely proportional to the order quantity—they decrease if the order quantity increases.

If order size is small, the average inventory is low and holding costs are low. However, a small order size requires frequent placement of orders and higher order placement costs. If order size is increased in an effort to reduce order placement costs, the average inventory levels increase and the holding costs increase. The economic order quantity reflects the trade-off between order placement costs and holding costs.

Reorder point is the lead time multiplied by the average daily demand. $R = d \times L$, where d is the average daily demand and L is the lead time (time between order placement and receipt of shipment).

The main assumptions used in the fixed quantity model are:

1. Demand for the product is constant and uniform.
2. Lead time is constant.
3. Order placement cost is constant.
4. Holding cost is based on average inventory.
5. Each order is received in a single delivery.
6. No back orders are allowed.

13.6 EOQ with Quantity Discount

When quantity discounts are offered to induce companies to buy in large quantities, a company must make a trade-off between reduced purchase price and higher inventory holding costs. Purchasing large quantities results in fewer orders, less order placement costs, and higher average inventory.

If unit holding costs do not change with the size of the order, EOQ remains the same for all ranges of the purchase price. However, if unit holding costs are expressed as a percentage of the purchase price (e.g., holding cost per year for one unit of item A is 20% of the purchase price for one unit of A), different prices result in different EOQs. Lower holding costs lead to larger EOQs.

In the presence of a quantity discount, a method to determine the optimal quantity for placing an order that minimizes total cost is as follows:

1. Start with the lowest price. Calculate EOQ for each price range until the EOQ falls in the quantity range for its price.
2. For the lowest price, if the EOQ falls in the quantity range, it is the optimal order quantity. If the EOQ is not in the lowest

price range, compare the total cost for the EOQ at its price range with the total cost at all the lower price ranges. The quantity that provides the lowest total cost is the optimal order quantity.

13.7   Safety Stock/Service Level

Safety stock is the inventory held in excess of expected demand to protect from stock-outs. To put it another way, safety stock (B) = reorder point (R) – average demand during lead time $(d \times L)$.

Service level is expressed in various ways, such as:

1. Probability of not running out of stock in any one inventory cycle.

2. Proportion of annual demand filled from stock.

3. Number of stock-outs tolerated per year.

4. Proportion of days in a year when an item is not out of stock.

13.8   Fixed-Time-Period Model

The fixed-time-period model is used to place orders for varying quantities at fixed time intervals. This model may be described as follows:

Place an order equal to $(T + P - A)$ units, where T is the target inventory, P is the safety stock, and A is the amount of inventory on hand at reorder time. Orders are triggered by time in this model. Order size is determined using the following equation:

$$q = d(I + L) + z\sigma_{T+L} - A$$

where q is the order size, d is the average daily demand, I is the time between orders, L is the lead time (time between placing an order and receiving the shipment), z is the number of standard deviations for a specified service level, and σ_{T+L} is the standard deviation of demand over the time between reviews and lead time:

$$\sigma_{T+L} = \sigma_d \sqrt{T + L}$$

CHAPTER 14

Material Requirements Planning

Material Requirements Planning (MRP) refers to a computer-based information system for managing dependent demand inventories and for scheduling replenishment orders. MRP starts with a schedule for finished goods and translates it into a schedule of requirements for components, raw materials, and sub-assemblies to determine what is needed, when it is needed, and how much is needed. MRP systems deliver the following advantages:

1. Reduced inventory levels.

2. Better customer service.

3. Reduced setup costs and reduced idle time.

4. Better response to market demands.

5. Ability to price more competitively.

6. Help in capacity planning.

7. Ability to track material requirements.

14.1 MRP Inputs

The three main inputs to MRP processing are the master schedule, bill of materials, and inventory records file.

1. *Master schedule* is a time-phased plan that provides a list of end items to be produced, the times when they are needed, and quantities. For example, a master schedule may indicate that 50 units of end item P are needed at the start of week 3 (as in the table below).

Item P	Week 1	Week 2	Week 3	Week 4	Week 5	Week 6
Quantity			50			75

The planning horizon used for a master schedule is divided into a series of time periods called *time buckets*, which are often expressed in weeks. The quantities shown in a master schedule are derived from various sources, such as customer orders, orders from warehouses, and forecasts.

Changes to quantities or times are managed to maintain stability. A series of time intervals called *time fences* are established and operational rules are developed. The nearest time fences are generally frozen (or fixed) to restrict changes; the farthest time fences are flexible (open) and permit changes. The time fences between the two extremes are considered moderate, allowing changes in specific products as long as the parts are available.

2. *Bill of Materials (BOM)* provides a complete product description and a listing of all the parts, raw materials, subassemblies, and assemblies that are needed to produce one unit of a finished product. It also describes the sequence of production steps required to create the finished product. The listing is hierarchical, showing the parts and quantities needed to produce a parent item. A *product structure tree* is a graphical technique for displaying the parts and requirements in a bill of materials. The requirements are listed by level: items at each level are components of the next level up and are parents of their components. *Low-level coding* is a restructuring of the bill of materials so that all occurrences of the component are made to coincide with the lowest level in which it appears.

3. *Inventory records file* contains information on the detail of each item, such as the supplier of the item, lead times, lot sizes, gross requirements, scheduled receipts, and amount on hand.

14.2   MRP Outputs

A broad range of reports, which are classified into primary and secondary reports, can be produced with an MRP system.

Primary reports are used for production and inventory planning and control. These include:

1. Planned orders—amount and timing of order releases at a future time.

2. Order releases—authorization for execution of planned orders.

3. Changes to planned orders—revision of due dates or quantities of orders or cancellations.

Secondary reports deal with performance control, planning, and exception. These include:

1. Performance reports—for evaluating system performance, deviation from plans, and costs.

2. Exception reports—to report major discrepancies, late or overdue orders, excessive scrap rates, etc.

14.3   MRP Processing

MRP processing uses the inputs to determine "time-phased requirements" for parts, raw materials, and sub-assemblies. MRP processing requires the following information.

Lot size ordering policy refers to the size of an order issued in the planned order receipts and planned order releases by MRP. Two common ordering policies are:

1. Lot-for-lot policy sets the planned order size equal to the net requirements.

2. Lot size policy sets the planned order size to a multiple of a pre-set lot size.

Lead time is the amount of time between the issuance of an order and receipt of the shipment from the supplier.

Gross requirements refer to total expected demand for an item during each time period generated using the master schedule and bill of materials, without regard to the inventory on hand. The quantity is derived from the master schedule for end items, and the quantity for components is derived from planned order releases of their immediate parents.

Schedule receipts refer to orders scheduled to be received from the suppliers.

Projected inventory on hand refers to the expected amount of inventory that will be on hand at the beginning of each time period (amount from prior period + scheduled receipts).

Net requirements are the actual amount of materials needed in a given time period (gross requirements – projected inventory on hand).

Planned order receipts refer to the quantity expected to be received at the beginning of a given time period.

Planned order releases refer to a planned amount to be ordered in a given time period. This is equal to planned order receipts offset by lead time.

A common format used for MRP processing is shown in the following table. (The columns following the description refers to units of time.) The purpose of the table is to show the format only.

Lot size = Lead time =	1	2	3	4	5
Gross requirements					
Scheduled receipts					
Projected inventory on hand					
Net requirements					
Planned order receipts					
Planned order releases					

14.4 Updating MRP Systems

MRP records are updated using two basic approaches: regenerative and net change. A *regenerative system* compiles all changes that occur within a particular time interval (week) and periodically updates the system. A *net change system* updates the MRP records continuously to reflect only the changes as they occur. A regenerative system is suitable for a system that is fairly stable, whereas a net change system is suitable for systems that have frequent changes.

14.5 MRP II

MRP II refers to manufacturing resources planning, which expands the scope of production resource planning to involve other functional areas of the firm, such as marketing and finance. The intent of MRP II is to integrate all the functions of the firm. The rationale for integrating the functional areas is the increased likelihood of developing an integrated plan that will work and which every department in the firm can tolerate.

CHAPTER 15

Scheduling

Scheduling refers to the allocation of resources, such as labor, facilities, and equipment, to accomplish specific tasks over time. Scheduling decisions are made at the final stage of the production process. A schedule is a "timetable" for performing activities, utilizing resources, and allocating resources.

The overall objective of scheduling is to achieve a trade-off among multiple and conflicting objectives, such as minimization of customer waiting time, minimization of inventories, minimization of production times, maximization of utilization of staff, equipment and facilities, and minimization of setup time. In a broad sense, scheduling is classified into workforce scheduling and operations scheduling.

15.1   Workforce Scheduling

Workforce scheduling deals with assigning resources (such as nurses or machinists) to specific workdays and shifts. It involves the translation of the staffing plan into specific work schedules for each employee. (See Chapter 12, Aggregate Planning.)

The objective is to generate a work schedule that minimizes the amount of total slack capacity while meeting the employee requirements and dealing with legal, behavioral, and psychological constraints.

A *rotating schedule* rotates employees through a series of work-days and/or hours. A *fixed schedule* requires an employee to work the same days and hours each week. Generating a work schedule for full-time and part-time employees in the presence of multiple shifts is a complex problem requiring specialized techniques such as linear programming. Even scheduling workers on a single shift basis can be a complicated task. A common workforce scheduling problem (without multiple shifts) involves developing a schedule which offers each employee two consecutive days off while still meeting the daily total employee requirement and minimizing the amount of slack capacity (i.e., the difference between total employees and the required number of employees).

In creating a schedule, one should first identify the constraints or requirements to be met. In this case the requirements are as follows:

1. Each employee requires two consecutive days off.

2. Each day's employee requirements must be met.

3. The slack capacity for each day should be as low as possible (i.e., minimized).

Different schedules can be derived based on the priority that these constraints hold in relation to each other.

Following are three sample work schedules, planned with the same constraints, but different priorities, in mind. Other work schedule scenarios can be worked out which produce the same overall results.

Rows labeled "# still needed" list the remaining number of employees required for that day before the next employee is added to the schedule. In the rows labeled "Employee #," the "X" denotes days the employee is scheduled to work; the "—" denotes days the employee is off. For each "X," one is subtracted from that day's requirement. The totals section at the bottom of the chart should be used to determine if the requirements for each day have been met, as well as each day's slack capacity.

In Schedule A, the first priority is to fill each day's worker

Schedule A

	Mon.	Tues.	Wed.	Thurs.	Fri.	Sat.	Sun.
Requirement	4	3	4	2	3	1	2
Employee 1	X	X	X	X	X	—	—
# still needed	3	2	3	1	2	1	2
Employee 2	X	X	X	X	—	—	X
# still needed	2	1	2	0	2	1	1
Employee 3	X	X	X	X	X	—	—
# still needed	1	0	1	0	1	1	1
Employee 4	—	—	X	X	X	X	X
# still needed	1	0	0	0	0	0	0
Employee 5	X	X	X	—	—	X	X
# still needed	0	0	0	0	0	0	0
Total Employees	4	4	5	4	3	2	3
# Required	4	3	4	2	3	1	2
Slack Capacity	0	1	1	2	0	1	1

requirements with days off to be scheduled for pairs of days in which the individual days have the least number of workers required.

When the first employee is scheduled, his days off are slated for Saturday and Sunday, the days requiring the least number of workers. When Employee 1 is deducted from the daily requirements for the week, three pairs of days become tied for the least number of workers required. Thursday–Friday, Friday–Saturday, and Saturday–Sunday are all pairs requiring one person for one day and two for the other. In this case Employee 2 is scheduled to have off on Friday and Saturday. For Employee 3, the pair with the least number of workers required becomes Saturday–Sunday, each day needing only one worker. Wednesday–Thursday or Thursday–Friday may seem like alternate choices, because as a pair, they also only require two workers.

65

However, since the requirement is that each day in the pair requires the least number of workers, Saturday–Sunday (requiring only one worker each) is a more appropriate pair, even though Thursday requires no workers to be scheduled at all. This pattern of scheduling and deduction continues until the remaining two workers are scheduled.

The totals at the bottom of the chart show that each day's requirements have been met.

Schedule B

	Mon.	Tues.	Wed.	Thurs.	Fri.	Sat.	Sun.
Requirement	4	3	4	2	3	1	2
Employee 1	X	X	X	X	X	—	—
# still needed	3	2	3	1	2	1	2
Employee 2	X	X	X	X	X	—	—
# still needed	2	1	2	0	1	1	2
Employee 3	X	X	X	X	X	—	—
# still needed	1	0	1	0	0	1	2
Employee 4	X	X	X	—	—	X	X
# still needed	0	0	0	0	0	0	1
Employee 5	X	X	X	—	—	X	X
# still needed	0	0	0	0	0	0	0
Total Employees	5	5	5	3	3	2	2
# Required	4	3	4	2	3	1	2
Slack Capacity	1	2	1	1	0	1	0

In Schedule B, the first priority is also to fill each day's worker requirements, but with no set priority as to how the days off are assigned. Thus, the workdays are filled in order, leaving the off-days to the end of the week. The first three workers are scheduled to be off on Saturday and Sunday. However, by the fourth employee, the

66

requirements for Saturday and Sunday have not been met. So, for Employees 4 and 5, the days off are shifted to a pair of days for which the requirements have already been met.

The totals at the bottom of the chart show that the requirements for each day have been met. Though in a different order, the breakdown of slack capacity remains essentially the same as in Schedule A, two days of zero slack capacity; one day of two; and for the rest of the days, a slack capacity of one.

Schedule C

	Mon.	Tues.	Wed.	Thurs.	Fri.	Sat.	Sun.
Requirement	4	3	4	2	3	1	2
Employee 1	—	—	X	X	X	X	X
# still needed	4	3	3	1	2	0	1
Employee 2	X	X	—	—	X	X	X
# still needed	3	2	3	1	1	0	0
Employee 3	X	X	X	X	—	—	X
# still needed	2	1	2	0	1	0	0
Employee 4	X	X	X	X	X	—	—
# still needed	1	0	1	0	0	0	0
Employee 5	X	X	X	—	—	X	X
# still needed	0	0	0	0	0	0	0
Total Employees	4	4	4	3	3	3	4
# Required	4	3	4	2	3	1	2
Slack Capacity	0	1	0	1	0	2	2

Schedule C places consecutive days off as the top priority, with the added directive that off-days be staggered so that not too many people are away from the business at one time. This schedule assigns the weekends first, filling in the requirements after. While this does produce a schedule in which no more than two people are out on any given day, it also creates an extra day when the slack capacity is two. This may not be desirable and is a factor to consider when arranging a schedule.

There are several techniques for generating workforce schedules ranging from the simple ones mentioned above to linear programming for complex schedules. Factors that increase the complexity of generating a workforce schedule include: large number of workers, combination of part-time and full-time workers, multiple shifts, labor union and government regulations, wide range of tasks and skills required, work performed by one employee dependent on work done by another employee, allocation of vacation, use of overtime work and sub-contractors, etc.

These techniques help an operations manager in making a trade-off between the cost of capacity and customer service level by adjusting the slack capacity. Slack capacity refers to the number of workers available in excess of the requirement. It protects from uncertainty in customer demand levels and employee attendance. For example, if there is a surge in the number of customers at a service facility, or, if an employee is absent from work due to sickness, the slack capacity helps fill the void created in the worker requirements. A high level of slack capacity results in better customer service, but leads to poor utilization and increased costs (salaries for additional workers, rent for increased office space, equipment such as computer terminals, etc.). A lower level of slack capacity generates lower operating costs, but results in poorer customer service. A low level of slack capacity is suitable for an operation with stable work (scheduling secretaries in an office), while a high level of slack capacity is suitable for operations with an uncertain demand and a large number of workers (scheduling check-out clerks at a large grocery store).

15.2   Operations Scheduling

Operations scheduling deals with the technical constraints directly related to production and serves the following functions:

1.   Allocating orders or jobs to workcenters (loading or assignment problem).

2. Specifying the sequence in which jobs are processed at the workcenter (sequencing problem).

3. Initiating work at the workcenters (dispatching problem).

4. Monitoring and controlling the progress of jobs and adjusting schedules.

Scheduling activities depend on the production volume of an operation.

High-volume operations (assembly line) are characterized by a smooth flow of parts through the production system or customers through the service system in order to achieve a high utilization of resources. Due to the highly repetitive nature of production, work is routed through a fixed sequence of workcenters. The allocation of tasks to workcenters and determination of the sequence of tasks are achieved through line balancing. Scheduling decisions in this type of operation are made during the design of the production process.

In *intermediate-volume operations* (batch production) scheduling decisions are based on the run size of the job, customer orders, and inventory levels. Scheduling issues are often addressed by models such as EOQ or MRP.

Low-volume operations (job-shop operation) scheduling is fairly complex due to the variability in processing requirements and materials. Since a wide variety of products is produced, general purpose machines are used to process orders with a variety of methods.

15.3 Loading/Assignment Problem

Loading refers to the assignment of jobs to workcenters with objectives, such as minimization of setup and processing costs, maximization of utilization, and minimization of job completion time. There are a number of methods for generating an assignment, ranging from pure intuition to linear programming. Two widely used methods are the Gantt chart and the assignment method.

The *Gantt chart* is a visual aid for organizing and clarifying the actual and intended use of resources over time. The horizontal scale is used to show time, and the resources are shown on the vertical scale. The jobs and their progress are shown in the body of the chart. The disadvantages of the Gantt chart are that it is not suitable for large numbers of jobs or for jobs with complex relationships.

The *assignment method* (also called the Hungarian method) is a simple procedure for generating optimal matching of jobs to workcenters that provide maximum profit, minimum cost, or minimum time. It starts with a table with rows representing the jobs, and columns representing workcenters or machines. A number in each cell of the table refers to criteria such as cost, profit, and time. This method involves the following steps:

1. Find the smallest number in each row and subtract it from every number in the row. Enter the results in a new table.

2. Find the smallest number in each column and subtract it from every number in the column. Enter the results in a new table.

3. Check if there is a zero in each row and column. Draw the minimum number of lines through the rows and columns that contain zeros. If the number of lines and number of rows are equal, go to Step 5. Otherwise, go to Step 4.

4. Find the smallest number in the cells that is not covered by the lines drawn in Step 3. Subtract this number from all the uncovered numbers in the table and add it to the numbers at the intersection of the lines. Go to Step 3.

5. Make assignments. Start with rows or columns with only one zero. Match jobs with the workcenters that have a zero cost. This gives a one-to-one matching of the jobs to workcenters. Using this assignment, go to the original table and add the costs to obtain the total cost as a result of the assignment.

EXAMPLE

The original table that follows shows the cost for processing jobs 1, 2, 3, and 4 on workcenters A, B, C, and D. The following steps show how an optimal matching of jobs to workcenters that minimizes total cost can be generated using the Hungarian method.

Original Table

WORKCENTERS

		A	B	C	D	Row Min
J	1	8	6	2	4	2
O	2	6	7	11	10	6
B	3	3	5	7	6	3
	4	5	10	12	9	5

The *first step* in the method is to find the smallest number in each row (2, 6, 3, 5 shown in the last column of the original table) and subtract it from each number in the corresponding row. The result is shown in the Step 1 Table. The revised cost in the first cell of the Step 1 Table is $8 - 2 = 6$.

Step 1 Table

WORKCENTERS

		A	B	C	D
J	1	6	4	0	2
O	2	0	1	5	4
B	3	0	2	4	3
	4	0	5	7	4
Column. Min.		0	1	0	2

The *second step* involves finding the smallest number in each column of the Step 1 Table (0, 1, 0, 2 shown in the last row of the Step 1 Table). The Step 2 Table is generated by subtracting these column minimums from each number in the corresponding columns.

Step 2 Table

WORKCENTERS

		A	B	C	D
J	1	6	3	0	0
O	2	0	0	5	2
B	3	0	1	4	1
	4	0	4	7	2

71

The *third step* involves drawing the least number of lines through rows or columns to cover all zeros in the table (dashed lines through rows 1 and 2 and column 1). Since the number of the lines is not equal to the number of rows in the table, continue with Step 4.

Step 3 Table

WORKCENTERS

		A	B	C	D
	1	6	3	0	0
J	2	0	0	5	2
O B	3	0	1	4	1
	4	0	4	7	2

In the *fourth step*, find the smallest number among the numbers not covered by the lines (1 is the smallest number in the box with 6 numbers not covered by the lines); then subtract it from the numbers not covered by lines, and add it to the numbers at the intersection of the lines.

Step 4 Table

WORKCENTERS

		A	B	C	D
	1	7	3	0	0
J	2	1	0	5	2
O B	3	0	0	3	0
	4	0	3	6	1

Then, repeating step 3, draw the least number of lines that cover all the zeros in the table (dashed lines through rows 1 and 3, and columns 1 and 2).

Next Table

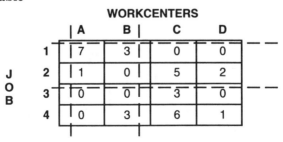

WORKCENTERS

		A	B	C	D
	1	7	3	0	0
J	2	1	0	5	2
O B	3	0	0	3	0
	4	0	3	6	1

At this point, the number of lines equals the number of rows, indicating that a solution is available. The zeros in the "Last Table" (with the boxes) help in finding the optimal matching of jobs to workcenters. By starting the matching process with rows or columns with a single zero, job 2 is assigned to workcenter B and job 4 to workcenter A. Then, assign job 1 to workcenter C and job 3 to workcenter D. After making the assignments, find the associated costs in the original table. Processing job 1 on workcenter C requires $2, job 2 on workcenter B requires $7, job 3 on workcenter D requires $6, and job 4 on workcenter A requires $5, adding up to a *total cost* of 2 + 7 + 6 + 5 = $20.

Last Table

	WORKCENTERS			
	A	B	C	D
1	7	3	0	0
2	1	0	5	2
3	0	0	3	0
4	0	3	6	1

Original Table

	WORKCENTERS			
	A	B	C	D
1	8	6	2	4
2	6	7	11	10
3	3	5	7	6
4	5	10	12	9

15.4   Sequencing Problems

Sequencing deals with the ordering or sequencing of jobs waiting to be processed at a workcenter. To generate a sequence for the jobs waiting to be processed, priority rules, such as *FCFS (First-Come-First-Served)*, *SPT (Shortest Processing Time)*, and *EDD (Early Due*

Date) rules, are used. Information required to generate job sequences include a list of jobs, job processing time for each job, and the due date for each job.

FCFS—Jobs are processed in the sequence in which they arrive at the workcenter.

SPT—Jobs are processed based on their processing times, from the least time needed to the most time needed.

EDD—Jobs are processed based on the due dates, from the earliest due date to the latest.

Given the following information:

Job	Time (in days)	Due date (in days)
A	2	7
B	8	16
C	4	4
D	10	17
E	5	15
F	12	18

the sequences generated by these three rules would be:

FCFS	A-B-C-D-E-F
SPT	A-C-E-B-D-F
EDD	C-A-E-B-D-F

Common *performance measures* used to judge a sequence are:

1. Average completion time—the ratio between total flow time and total number of jobs processed.

2. Average job lateness—the ratio between total number of jobs late and total number of jobs processed.

3. Average number of jobs at the workcenter—the ratio between total flow time and total processing time.

4. Flow time—the cumulative processing time for a job.

This information is useful in evaluating sequences, establishing future delivery dates, and determining the levels of work-in-process inventory.

These rules assume that setup time is independent of the processing sequence. Due dates for jobs are based on delivery dates promised to the customers or by managerial decisions.

CHAPTER 16

Advanced Manufacturing

Advanced manufacturing technology, including group technology and flexible automation, developed as a result of problems faced by two types of production: mass production and batch production. *Mass production operations* have high equipment utilization, and parts are processed through a sequence of steps without delay. Shorter product life cycles and frequent changes to the product design make producing large volumes of the same product impractical. *Batch production operations* are capable of producing a variety of products in batches. However, there are significant delays and problems caused by organizing and handling different sets of tooling, different gauges and fixtures, different parts, and different process plans and drawings. Group technology and flexible automation try to capture the benefits of both types of production.

16.1 Group Technology

Group technology refers to the process of grouping parts with similar design and manufacturing characteristics. Group technology promotes streamlining, simplifying, and standardizing operations. Group technology capitalizes on similarities in three ways, by:

1. Performing similar activities together.

2. Standardizing closely related parts or activities.

3. Efficiently managing information related to recurring problems.

Advantages of group technology include:

1. Reduced production time.
2. Reduced inventories.
3. Reduced time for product design.
4. Reduced manufacturing and purchase costs.

Classification, family formation, simplification, and standardization are the underlying concepts of group technology.

1. *Classification* involves grouping parts together based on similarities. This step begins by determining measures that judge similarity (such as geometric similarity or process similarity).

2. *Family formation* is the process of selecting parts that fit a set of characteristics required for a specific purpose from a large population by considering multiple attributes.

3. *Simplification* involves reduction of unnecessary variety (design attributes and tooling) to reduce confusion and errors and to increase efficiency and speed.

4. *Standardization* involves selecting a best procedure and implementing it to increase efficiency and control.

Cellular manufacturing refers to the physical layout of a factory into product-oriented workcenters. Each workcenter consists of machines and tools necessary to efficiently produce a family of parts specified by group technology methods. The objectives of cellular manufacturing include reducing material handling time, simplifying tool control, reducing in-process inventory, and improving operator expertise.

16.2 Flexible Automation

A *Flexible Manufacturing System (FMS)* is comprised of flexible machines, usually integrated by a computer system, that are capable of processing different types of components without significant delays and human intervention. FMS systems have important advantages:

1. Ability to process new and different products with ease.

2. High equipment utilization because time between processing different parts is less.

3. Reduced equipment costs as each machine has greater productive output as a result of high utilization.

4. Improved market response as a result of shortened lead times.

5. Reduced direct labor costs, since part loading and unloading is centralized and requires fewer workers.

Implementation of FMS involves high initial investment, complexity, knowledgeable and supportive management, and an adaptable workforce. The commonly used approaches for designing these systems are linear programming, simulation, and queuing.

16.3 Other Advanced Manufacturing Methods

Computer Numerical Control (CNC) refers to the application of computer technology to numerically controlled machines, utilizing computer hardware and software to control machine operations. CNC reduces direct labor costs, improves product quality and precision, and reduces time to load NC software.

Computer-Aided Manufacturing (CAM) refers to the application of computer communications technology to enhance manufacturing by linking CNC machines, monitoring the production process, and providing automatic feedback to control operations. CAM provides benefits, such as:

1. Improving manufacturing control and reporting.

2. Enhancing coordination of material flow between machines.

3. Enhancing re-routing capabilities.

An *industrial robot* is a general-purpose programmable machine possessing certain human-like capabilities (such as grasping and sensing). The advantages of robots include:

1. Reducing direct labor costs.

2. Improving quality and precision in repetitive tasks.

3. Avoiding risk to humans in hazardous working conditions.

4. Increasing throughput.

Automated material handling systems include Automated Guided Vehicles (AGVs) and Automated Storage and Retrieval Systems (AS/RS) components. An AGV is a computerized cart system capable of delivering parts and tools to and from multiple workcenters. AGV may be used with an AS/RS, which is a computerized system for storing and retrieving parts and tools. Advantages of these systems include:

1. Reduced material handling costs.

2. Improved inventory control.

3. Improved safety and control of material movement.

4. Reduced work-in-process inventory on the shop floor.

Computer-Aided Process Planning (CAPP) is a decision support system which generates instructions for the production of parts. Based on information about machining requirements and machine capabilities, CAPP plans machining operations and determines routing between machines. The objectives of CAPP include:

1. Enabling manufacturing to cope with the complexity of process planning in a multiple-product environment.

2. Reducing the cost and effort required to create and revise process plans.

CHAPTER 17

Linear Programming

Linear Programming (LP) refers to a set of techniques that are useful for solving problems involving allocation of scarce resources among competing demands in an optimal manner. LP methods are used to solve a variety of operations management problems, such as capacity planning, assignment problems, transportation problems, and blending problems. These methods have been widely used to solve a number of industrial, military, economic, and social problems.

17.1 LP Model

The information about a decision problem is assembled into an LP model using four components:

1. *Objective function*—the intent of the model, such as maximizing profits, minimizing costs, and minimizing production time.

2. *Constraint functions*—limits on the available resources.

3. *Decision variables*—choices in terms of amounts of inputs or outputs.

4. *Parameters*—fixed values used in the model, such as unit costs or prices.

The model can be represented in different formats, such as an algebraic format or an industry-standard "MPS" format. A problem represented as an LP model can be solved using a variety of approaches, such as graphical linear programming (for problems with two decision variables), simplex method, and interior-point methods (for extremely large problems). Several computer software products, such as LINDO®, CPLEX®, and OSL®, are available to solve the LP models. The following chart is a sample algebraic LP model:

Objective function	Maximize profit: $2x_1 + 3x_2 + x_3$
Constraints	$x_1 + x_2 + x_3 \leq 300$ (labor constraint)
	$x_1 + 4x_2 + 7x_3 \leq 900$ (raw material constraint)
Variables	x_1, x_2, x_3
Parameters	2, 3, 1 (unit profits)
	1, 1, 1, 300 (labor hours)
	1, 4, 7, 900 (pounds of raw material)

17.2 LP Solution

The solution to an LP problem consists of the following information:

1. *Values of the decision variables*—provide an optimal solution.

2. *Objective function value*—derived by substituting the values of the decision variables in the objective function.

3. *Slack*—associated with each "≤" type of constraint. After substituting the values of variables in the constraint function, the difference between the right-hand side and the left-hand side of the equation gives the slack associated with the constraint.

4. *Surplus*—associated with each "≥" type of constraint. After

81

substituting the values of variables in the constraint function, the difference between the right-hand side and the left-hand side of the equation gives the surplus associated with the constraint.

5. *Shadow price*—associated with each constraint; indicates how change of one unit of resource represented by the constraint would change the value of the objective function.

6. *Reduced cost*—associated with each variable; indicates the amount by which its coefficient in the objective function can be changed without making the variable enter the solution.

17.3   Related Methods

Integer programming refers to a special class of problems and techniques involving decisions of a logical and countable nature. The decision variables are restricted to integer values. For example, a car rental company trying to decide on the number of cars to buy and lease may formulate the problem using integer programming and expect the decision variables to take integer values, indicating the number of cars to buy or lease.

Nonlinear programming is used if an objective function and/or any constraint function is nonlinear. *Multiple-objective programming* refers to handling more than one objective in solving the above problems. For example, instead of solving a problem to minimize cost only, this class of problems involves consideration of more objectives, such as maximization of machine utilization, minimization of time, etc.

CHAPTER 18

Waiting-Line Management

Waiting-line management involves setting a level of capacity that minimizes the sum of the cost of service capacity and the cost of customers waiting in the line. The objectives of the waiting-line management problem are to minimize costs and maximize customer satisfaction levels. Customer satisfaction levels can be increased by reducing waiting lines and service times. This requires an increase in capacity (additional workers, equipment, facilities) resulting in increased capacity costs. On the other hand, the time spent by customers waiting in the line results in increased costs (salaries paid to employees while they wait and space requirements to hold waiting customers). The goal is to determine an optimum service capacity level that minimizes total costs.

18.1   Simulation and Queuing Analysis

Simulation and *queuing analysis* involve the design of a mathematical-logical model of a real system and experimenting with the model to evaluate the performance of a system. These models are useful in designing production processes, creating schedules, determining inventory levels, etc.

Basic steps in the simulation or queuing procedure are:

1.   Define the problem and objectives.

83

2. Build a model of the system using mathematical-logical relationships.

3. Specify, identify, and collect relevant data.

4. Prepare the model for computer processing.

5. Verify and validate to ensure the model reasonably resembles the real system.

6. Experiment with the model and analyze the results.

7. Implement the results obtained from the model, and document the process.

While simulation provides information on the dynamic behavior of the system, queuing models provide steady-state information.

18.2 Simulation

Simulation involves two steps which are generally performed on a computer. First, create the model. Then design, implement, and analyze experiments involving the model. The simulations help explain the relationship between variables in the system, how the variables impact the system performance, and the evaluation of design alternatives.

Simulation models provide information on a variety of performance measures. The performance of a system is measured by its effectiveness and efficiency in achieving goals. Important performance measures include:

1. Capacity measures (production rate and system capacity).

2. Measures describing the ability to meet deadlines.

3. Utilization measures.

4. In-process inventory measures.

The advantages of simulation include a clear and easy-to-understand pictorial or graphical representation of the system, and that experimentation can be performed without disturbing or destroying a real system. Simulation analysis can be performed using computer software products such as SLAM® and SIMAN®.

18.3 Queuing

Queuing models involve the use of mathematical approaches to analyze waiting-line problems. Queuing models help an operations manager to achieve a trade-off between the cost of providing a level of service capacity and the cost of a customer waiting for service.

The main characteristics of a queuing model are:

1. *Population source*—which is classified into *infinite source situation*, where the number of potential customers far exceeds the system capacity and is considered infinite (toll bridges, supermarkets); and *finite source situation*, where the number of customers is limited (number of patients waiting for a nurse in a hospital).

2. *Number of servers*—either a single server (single bay car wash) or multiple servers (gas stations).

3. *Arrival and service patterns (rates)*—this pattern may follow any statistical distribution. Most commonly used models assume that the arrival rate is described by Poisson distribution and the service time is described by negative exponential distribution.

4. *Queue discipline*—order in which customers are processed.

There are several types of queuing models. Most models are based on two items of information—arrival rate (λ) and service rate (μ). Commonly used performance measures are utilization rate, average number of customers waiting, and average waiting time.

Performance measures for a simple model consisting of a single server, Poisson arrival rate, exponential service time, an FCFS (First-Come-First-Served) order discipline, and infinite population source are shown in the following table:

85

Performance measure	Formula
Utilization	$\rho = \dfrac{\lambda}{\mu}$
Average number of customers waiting in the line	$n_l = \dfrac{\lambda^2}{\mu(\mu - \lambda)}$
Average number of customers in the system	$n_s = \dfrac{\lambda}{(\mu - \lambda)}$
Average waiting time in the line	$t_l = \dfrac{\lambda}{\mu(\mu - \lambda)}$
Average waiting time in the system	$t_s = \dfrac{1}{(\mu - \lambda)}$

CHAPTER 19

Materials, Purchasing, and Maintenance

19.1   Materials Management

Material handling is concerned with all aspects of the flow of materials within an organization—from the receiving area, through production stages, to the final shipment stage. Material handling is an integral part of production in all manufacturing organizations and an important concern in the operation of most wholesalers, distributors, and retailers. The main objectives of material handling include:

1. Minimizing travel distance.

2. Minimizing goods in process.

3. Removing bottlenecks and ensuring smooth flow.

4. Minimizing losses from waste, breakage, spoilage, and theft.

Inputs to material handling are derived from demands originating from the physical supply, production, and distribution functions. The inputs are provided by methods such as flow analysis, which uses symbols and charts to represent the features of a procedure. Materials are classified into: bulk materials (stone, wheat, petroleum, etc.), itemized material (discrete parts and components), and unitized material (containers and pallets). Material-handling decisions are subject to constraints such as:

1. *Flowability*—affinity of materials and process characteristics to flow requirements.

2. *Movement dimensions*—quantifying the flow of material (distance, direction, intensity, and space).

3. *Costs*—direct *material-handling costs* (equipment, labor, maintenance, operating) and *indirect material-handling costs* (equipment and labor downtime, opportunity, and overhead).

Flow factors are considerations other than constraints that influence material-handling decisions. They include movement features describing the variability of material flow, unitization concerned with methods for enhancing material flowability, and equipment alternatives encompassing a vast array of hardware available to meet the handling requirements.

Outputs of material-handling decisions provide insight into the achievement of various objectives. The primary outputs of these decisions deal with handling efficiencies (minimizing material handling, minimizing unit load size, minimizing idle time, moving larger weights over shorter distances) and sourcing (refers to methods for obtaining resources for material handling).

Design of material-handling systems includes the following phases:

1. Define the objectives/scope of the material-handling system.

2. Analyze the handling, storage, and control requirements.

3. Generate alternate material-handling system designs.

4. Evaluate alternate material-handling system designs.

5. Select and implement the preferred material-handling system design.

19.2   Purchasing Management

Purchasing refers to the exchange of money for goods or services, and procurement refers to the total responsibility of acquiring goods and services necessary for an organization. The ability of the purchasing function to obtain the required materials, equipment, services, and supplies at the right prices and at the right time is a key to successful operations.

Inputs to the purchasing decision are purchase requisitions and product specifications. Constraints and factors influencing the purchasing decision include legal considerations, management policies, resource limitations, cultural influences, market conditions, and demand factors. The output of the purchasing function includes the selected supplier, price, time of purchase, and an awarded contract. Information valuable to making purchasing decisions includes the following:

1. List of supply sources.

2. Appraisal of supplier performance.

3. Cost and price data.

4. Database for make/buy/lease decisions.

5. Evaluation of purchasing agent's effectiveness.

19.3   Maintenance Management

Maintenance management refers to the function responsible for keeping and restoring assets to satisfactory operating status. It is primarily concerned with plant, machinery, and equipment. It involves tasks such as replacing worn-out parts and components, servicing equipment, keeping up buildings, and handling emergency repairs. Two important types of maintenance are: *breakdown maintenance*—no action is taken until an asset has failed—and *preventive maintenance*—action is designed to delay or prevent breakdowns.

Typical breakdown costs include the cost of repairs, equipment downtime, idle labor, loss of production output, schedule delays, and customer dissatisfaction. The objectives of maintenance are to prevent breakdowns and minimize total costs.

Preventive maintenance yields several benefits, which include:

1. Reducing maintenance costs.

2. Performing maintenance whenever convenient.

3. Providing ability to contract maintenance.

4. Reducing spare parts inventory.

5. Reducing overtime and standby equipment required.

CHAPTER 20

Decision Making

Decision making is a fundamental process of operations management and other functional areas of management. The decision-making process generally includes the following steps:

1. Identify the problem (the root problem, not the symptoms).
2. Identify the objectives by which proposed solution alternatives will be judged.
3. Develop solution alternatives.
4. Analyze and compare solution alternatives using mathematical techniques.
5. Select the best solution alternative based on the specified objectives.
6. Implement the selected solution.
7. Monitor the results to ensure that the desired results are obtained.

Suboptimization refers to each different department attempting to obtain results that are optimum to itself. A solution that is optimal to a department may not be optimal for the organization as a whole, resulting in suboptimization.

A *payoff table* (as the following example shows) is a useful format for summarizing the information related to a decision problem. It shows the expected payoffs for each alternative under various scenarios. The likelihood of occurrence of each scenario may be estimated using probabilities. The payoff table places all alternatives in a format that is easy for comparison.

Alternative	Demand		
	High	**Medium**	**Low**
A	100	100	100
B	150	150	80
C	200	75	-20

20.1　Decision Environments

Decisions can be classified into three categories based on the degree of certainty present in the decision environment:

1. *Certainty*—environment in which relevant parameters such as costs, resource availability, and demand have known values (e.g., demand is known).

2. *Uncertainty*—environment in which it is not possible to assess the likelihood of future events (e.g., demand is unknown).

3. *Risk*—environment in which some parameters have probabilistic outcomes (e.g., demand is probabilistic: 50% high demand, 30% medium demand, 20% low demand).

20.2　Decision Making Approaches

A decision approach should correspond with the decision environment.

Decision making under certainty—If all relevant parameters are known, decision making is straightforward. Select the alternative that provides the best payoff.

Decision making under uncertainty—Under conditions of unknown future events, four approaches may be used:

1. *Maximax*—Find the best payoff for each alternative and select the alternative which has the best possible payoff.

2. *Maximin*—Find the worst payoff for each alternative and select the alternative which has the best among the worst payoffs.

3. *Laplace*—Find the average payoff for each alternative and select the alternative with the best average payoff. Pierre Laplace, the French mathematician known for his work on the theory of probabilities, argued that "knowing nothing at all about the true state of nature" is equivalent to "all states having equal probability." Laplace's line of reasoning justifies selection of an alternative based on average value.

4. *Minimax regret*—Find the worst regret for each alternative and choose the alternative with the best among the worst regrets. (Regret is the difference between a given payoff and the best payoff in the same column of the payoff table.)

Decision making under risk: When the probability of the occurrence of future events can be estimated, it is possible to calculate all expected monetary values for each alternative, and the alternative with the best expected monetary value can be selected. The expected value of perfect information refers to the difference between the expected payoff under certainty and the expected payoff under risk.

Areas of the Cumulative Standard Normal Distribution*

z	G(z)	z	G(z)	z	G(z)	z	G(z)
-4.00	0.00003	-1.95	0.02559	0.10	0.53983	2.15	0.98422
-3.95	0.00004	-1.90	0.02872	0.15	0.55962	2.20	0.98610
-3.90	0.00005	-1.85	0.03216	0.20	0.57926	2.25	0.98778
-3.85	0.00006	-1.80	0.03593	0.25	0.59871	2.30	0.98928
-3.80	0.00007	-1.75	0.04006	0.30	0.61791	2.35	0.99061
-3.75	0.00009	-1.70	0.04457	0.35	0.63683	2.40	0.99180
-3.70	0.00011	-1.65	0.04947	0.40	0.65542	2.45	0.99286
-3.65	0.00013	-1.60	0.05480	0.45	0.67364	2.50	0.99379
-3.60	0.00016	-1.55	0.06057	0.50	0.69146	2.55	0.99461
-3.55	0.00019	-1.50	0.06681	0.55	0.70884	2.60	0.99534
-3.50	0.00023	-1.45	0.07353	0.60	0.72575	2.65	0.99598
-3.45	0.00028	-1.40	0.08076	0.65	0.74215	2.70	0.99653
-3.40	0.00034	-1.35	0.08851	0.70	0.75804	2.75	0.99702
-3.35	0.00040	-1.30	0.09680	0.75	0.77337	2.80	0.99744
-3.30	0.00048	-1.25	0.10565	0.80	0.78814	2.85	0.99781
-3.25	0.00058	-1.20	0.11507	0.85	0.80234	2.90	0.99813
-3.20	0.00069	-1.15	0.12507	0.90	0.81594	2.95	0.99841
-3.15	0.00082	-1.10	0.13567	0.95	0.82894	3.00	0.99865
-3.10	0.00097	-1.05	0.14686	1.00	0.84134	3.05	0.99886
-3.05	0.00114	-1.00	0.15866	1.05	0.85314	3.10	0.99903
-3.00	0.00135	-0.95	0.17106	1.10	0.86433	3.15	0.99918
-2.95	0.00159	-0.90	0.18406	1.15	0.87493	3.20	0.99931
-2.90	0.00187	-0.85	0.19766	1.20	0.88493	3.25	0.99942
-2.85	0.00219	-0.80	0.21186	1.25	0.89435	3.30	0.99952
-2.80	0.00256	-0.75	0.22663	1.30	0.90320	3.35	0.99960
-2.75	0.00298	-0.70	0.24196	1.35	0.91149	3.40	0.99966
-2.70	0.00347	-0.65	0.25785	1.40	0.91924	3.45	0.99972
-2.65	0.00402	-0.60	0.27425	1.45	0.92647	3.50	0.99977
-2.60	0.00466	-0.55	0.29116	1.50	0.93319	3.55	0.99981
-2.55	0.00539	-0.50	0.30854	1.55	0.93943	3.60	0.99984
-2.50	0.00621	-0.45	0.32636	1.60	0.94520	3.65	0.99987
-2.45	0.00714	-0.40	0.34458	1.65	0.95053	3.70	0.99989
-2.40	0.00820	-0.35	0.36317	1.70	0.95543	3.75	0.99991
-2.35	0.00939	-0.30	0.38209	1.75	0.95994	3.80	0.99993
-2.30	0.01072	-0.25	0.40129	1.80	0.96407	3.85	0.99994
-2.25	0.01222	-0.20	0.42074	1.85	0.96784	3.90	0.99995
-2.20	0.01390	-0.15	0.44038	1.90	0.97128	3.95	0.99996
-2.15	0.01578	-0.10	0.46017	1.95	0.97441	4.00	0.99997
-2.10	0.01786	-0.05	0.48006	2.00	0.97725		
-2.05	0.02018	0.00	0.50000	2.05	0.97982		
-2.00	0.02275	0.05	0.51994	2.10	0.98214		

* generated using Microsoft EXCEL Version 5. 0

G(z) corresponds to the proportion under the curve cumulated from the negative tail.

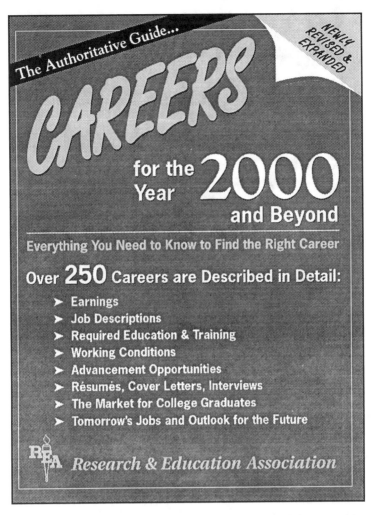